Can I Play You My Song?

▲▲▲▲▲▲▲▲▲▲▲▲▲▲▲▲▲▲▲▲▲

Can I Play You
My Song?

▲▲▲▲▲▲▲▲▲▲▲▲▲▲ The Compositions and
Invented Notations of Children

Rena Upitis ▪▪▪▪▪▪▪▪▪

Queen's University
Kingston, Ontario

With a Foreword by
Glenda L. Bissex

 HEINEMANN
Portsmouth, New Hampshire

Heinemann Educational Books, Inc.
361 Hanover Street Portsmouth, NH 03801
Offices and agents throughout the world

The author and publisher wish to thank the following for permission to reprint previously published material appearing in this book:

Figure 1–10 (top): From *The Notation of Western Music* by Richard Rastall. New York: St. Martin's Press, 1982, p. 255. Used by permission of Belmont Music Publishers, Pacific Palisades CA 90272.

Figure 1–10 (bottom): From *Style and Idea: Selected Writings*. Arnold Schoenberg, Leonard Stein, eds. Edited/translated by Leo Black. Copyright © 1975 Belmont Music Publishers. Used by permission of University of California Press and Faber & Faber.

Figure 3–6: From Davidson, L., Scripp, L., & Welsh, P. 1988. "Happy Birthday: Evidence for Conflicts of Perceptual Knowledge and Conceptual Understanding." *Journal of Aesthetic Education* 22, 65–74.

Figures 1–4, 1–7, 3–19, 4–10, 4–11, 5–2, 5–14, 5–15: All or part of these figures originally appeared in *This Too Is Music* copyright 1990 by Rena Upitis. Portsmouth, NH: Heinemann. Reprinted by permission.

Every effort has been made to contact the copyright holders and the children and their parents for permission to reprint borrowed material. We regret any oversights that may have occurred and would be happy to rectify them in future printings of this work.

Library of Congress Cataloging-in-Publication Data
Upitis, Rena Brigit.
    Can I play you my song? : the compositions and invented notations of children / Rena Upitis.
       p. cm.
    Includes bibliographical references.
    ISBN 0-435-08705-3
    1. Music—Instruction and study—Juvenile. 2. Composition (Music) 3. Musical notation.   I. Title.
MT742.U65 1992
372.87'4—dc20
                                             92-4674
                                               CIP
                                             MN

Back-cover photo © 1991 Sparks Studio, Kingston, Ontario.
Designed by Jenny Jensen Greenleaf.
Printed in the United States of America.
92 93 94 95 96 97   10 9 8 7 6 5 4 3 2 1

Contents

Foreword vii

Acknowledgments xi

1. "But I don't know how to read music—
   how can I teach it?" 1

2. Creating a Rich Music Setting 19

3. The Development of Children's Invented
   Music Notations 41

4. Interactions Between Performance
   and Notation 79

5. Enhancing Children's Invented Notations 103

6. A Whole Music Approach to Becoming
   a Musician 145

   Appendix A: Issues of General
   Cognitive Growth 153

   Appendix B: The Nursery Blues 163

   Glossary of Musical Terms 173

   References 183

▲ ▲

Foreword

Glenda L. Bissex

Who would have guessed twenty
years ago that invented spelling was anything but the special gift
of a few children of highly educated parents? Now children in
thousands of classrooms demonstrate what a universal human gift
it is, enabling them to write earlier, at greater length and with more
varied language than we thought possible. *Can I Play You My Song?*
suggests that invented musical notation may be another such gift,
opening a door to children's composing as invented spelling
opened a door to young children's writing. What an exciting area
this opens up for teachers and for teacher research!

The parallels Rena Upitis draws between whole language/process
writing approaches and her own approach to teaching music will
give many language arts teachers and their students some familiar
footing. They already know about audience awareness, conferences, revision, folders, and mini-lessons. Teachers who have
watched invented spellings evolve can expect to see similar phases
of growth in invented musical notations, as Upitis outlines them.
And teachers who have come to see students as writers will be

able to see them also as composers and will understand the importance of their making their own music.

As the research spearheaded by Donald Graves has shown, once we educators stop being concerned only with what we have to teach children, we can let children show us what they know. We may stand amazed at their knowledge rather than discouraged by their errors. When we drill children on conventions—whether sound-letter correspondences or spellings or math facts—we naturally tend to focus on their mistakes, a disheartening experience for both teachers and learners. When children are creating their own notation systems, the focus is more on what they *do* understand, not only the details but the powerful conceptual understandings, such as the possibility of representing sounds and meanings by little marks on paper that are part of a total system, or the nature of a sentence or of a musical phrase.

The growing emphasis on real writing, real literature, and, now, original music in classrooms transforms teaching from instruction by rituals in which we know the right answers and correct children's errors to participation in which we are challenged by the inventions and interpretations of children, in which we enjoy the reading and the writing and the music we share with students. Upitis's ideas for encouraging composing, improvising, and notation made me head straight for my piano. Why should the kids have all the fun?

Teachers need not know a great deal about standard musical notation to encourage learners to create their own for, as the many examples in this book show, the children's systems are usually more intuitive, more graphically representational than our standard system. And the "expert" on any particular system is right there to explain it. Children also learn from observing each other's notations since when we—children and adults alike—are creating, there are no single "right" answers a teacher can provide. A mathematically inclined child and I discovered that piano compositions of his encompassing a limited range of tones could be notated with Cuisenaire rods, their different lengths expressing different intervals, the ascending and descending and recurring patterns colorfully clear. Using these math manipulatives, he could compose starting from visual or mathematical patterns rather than from tones.

Fostering children's invented musical notations, as Upitis helps us to do, provides a foundation for them eventually to learn standard notation—a more creative, meaningful, and enjoyable way than my hours as a child at the piano with a keyboard chart, struggling by rote to learn a foreign language. When these children become readers of printed music, I imagine they'll know from their own composing experience that the music is more than the notes.

Some years ago I decided I might extend my understanding of composing with words by attempting to compose music. The process of revision was familiar enough through my research as well as my own practice in writing. What I didn't anticipate was the struggle with notation, humbling me to the position of a young would-be writer who knows the language, has some not so simple ideas to express, but doesn't yet know the writing system. Those years of piano lessons had taught me how to read standard notation—although not very well, I discovered—but they didn't prepare me to write music or to listen carefully enough to know everything to write down.

Until I sang the hymns of Hildegard of Bingen as written in her twelfth-century figural musical notation of squiggles, dots, and angles, often representing several notes at once, I couldn't imagine the advantages of a notation system other than the one I'd labored at the piano to learn. But my vocal group sang the hymns more flowingly from the original notation than from transcriptions in modern notation where every note was separately represented. Unlike later music, Hildegard's has no underlying beat—no time signature or bar lines, nothing to count; it moves forward in another way as the old notation suggests. Current concepts of "development" as progress toward perfection lead us to see both children and earlier notation systems as deficient. Yet our seeing them as deficient may reflect rather our failure to understand them in their own terms.

Why bother with the musical notations of children when hardly any of them will become professional composers? For the same reasons that we bother with children's writing although most of them will not become professional writers. Composing is a fundamental human activity, whether we compose with words, with blocks, with paint, or with tones. Behind this seemingly small matter of children's invented musical notation lies something bigger than whole music or whole language. It is more like whole mind: the human mind at work through symbol systems, which represent and also shape our perceptions, our worlds, both outer and inner. Giving access to the many languages of the human mind is the work of education.

▲▲▲▲▲▲▲▲▲▲▲▲▲▲▲▲▲▲▲▲▲▲▲▲▲▲▲▲▲▲

Acknowledgments

▲▲▲▲▲▲▲▲▲▲▲▲▲▲▲▲▲▲ THIS book has been long in the making, and so, has been influenced by a great many people. Sadly, I can no longer remember everyone who in some way contributed to the thoughts and stories related herein. But even if I could remember all of those children, friends, and colleagues that have been involved, it would take pages and pages to list them all. Nevertheless, I trust that I have represented them well, if not in name then in spirit.

My thanks to all of the children who have enriched my life through their eyes. Watching children create notations and make music inspired me to take on this kind of work, and their ingenuity continued to sustain me when the task of describing their creations seemed overwhelming.

I am lucky to work in a university community where my work is both supported and appreciated. Financial assistance from the Principal's Development Fund, Queen's University is gratefully acknowledged. Moreover, I am indebted to my colleagues at the Faculty of Education, Queen's University, and at the Media Lab, Massachusetts Institute of Technology, for the countless conversations we have had about children's notations. I also thank Lyle Davidson, of Harvard's Project Zero, for his valuable views and criticisms of my work over the past decade.

There are several people who helped significantly with the final stages of producing this book – reading drafts, collecting and sorting notation samples, proofreading, and offering suggestions for re-working difficult passages in the text. In particular, my heart-felt thanks to Julia du Prey and Gary Rasberry, both of whom made my work a part of theirs, and therefore contributed enormously to the end result.

And finally, my thanks to the tireless, dedicated staff of Heinemann. Working with the folks at Heinemann Educational Books has made the publishing process a pleasure.

"But I don't know how to read music—how can I teach it?"

▲ ▲ ▲ ▲ ▲ ▲ ▲ ▲ ▲ ▲ ▲ ▲ ▲ ▲ ▲ ▲ ▲   WHEN I first began talking with people about writing this book, I encountered two distinct responses. Eyes lit up for those who already knew how to read music, as they started to think about the many possibilities of children's compositions and notations that could be included in a book such as this. Others—those who didn't read music—were less enthusiastic. While they could understand the need for a serious look at children's music creations, they were not sure how they themselves could relate to such a book. So the first challenge in writing this book is to show those belonging to the latter group that this book is written for them, as well for those who already read standard notation.

    I strongly believe that many elementary teachers, even those who don't read music, can nevertheless teach children to read and write music, *as they learn along with their students*. But in order for this to happen, several conditions need to be present in the classroom setting. The first condition, and the most important as I see it, is that teachers who want children to compose and learn about music notation need to believe in, and practice, a learner-directed approach to teaching and learning. Such a learner-directed or child-centered approach is becoming more and more prevalent in elementary classrooms. These classrooms are characterized by several features. They include active exploration on the part of the students, the presence of many 'manipulable' materials, recognition and acceptance of children's original works, encouraging learners (including the teacher) to take intellectual risks and accept the errors that come with taking such risks, and generally, honoring children as learners. In this kind of setting, learning about all sorts of things—patterns of language, relationships in mathematics, laws of science—is not only possible, but natural. Learning about music notation can also happen through manipulation, exploration, and creation in a regular child-centered classroom. This is in sharp contrast to our traditional view of a music teacher ruling a **staff** on the blackboard and indicating to his or her less than enraptured students that F is found on the bottom space in the treble clef.[1]

Another important characteristic of teachers who are able and willing to teach music notation through the original work of children is their ability to see and share the magic and beauty in children's notations. Like the parent who delights in a child's early scribbling, we need to feel the same excitement for the music notations that children offer us. There are two notations reproduced in Figure 1–1, both produced by the same child, Joel, when he was four years old. Both were written for me—a family friend, and also the piano teacher for Joel's older sister and mother. The first is a letter, written when his mother had hurt her back and was confined to bed for some weeks and unable to practice the piano. However, she could play by propping a synthesizer across her lap. The second is an example of an analogous music scribble, in which Joel was writing music for me to play. The first is probably more familiar

---

[1] I have found that using music terminology like "staff" from the outset, rather than something like "those five straight lines," does not appear to confuse children, and in fact probably gives them a technical language to use far sooner than would otherwise be the case. I take the same approach in this book. However, should any of the terms used cause undue confusion, a glossary of terms can be found at the back of the book. Words defined in the glossary appear in bold face in the text when they are first used.

FIGURE I-I *Early scribbling — a letter and some music*

Dear Rena,

Thank you for bringing the sympathizer [synthesizer] and letting my Mommy play on her back.

Love, Joel

This is some music for you to play.

to most people than the second. But the point here is that they are remarkably similar. Both forms of writing were quite natural for Joel to make, for in his home he had seen many examples of print and of music. Further, he had already made the significant deduction that these forms of writing carried meaning for both the writer and receiver of the message, and that I would be able to read both, and show my appreciation and understanding in doing so.

When a parent sees a child make what to him or her is a meaningful scribble, it is second nature for the parent to encourage such scribbling, knowing that this encouragement is somehow part of the process of learning to write. If the same encouragement were given for the music scribbles, by parents and teachers both, would children not also learn to write music? This notion is developed at length in subsequent chapters.

When teaching music notation to children, it is also important to give them ways to relate their notations to instruments. Making and playing instruments is inextricably linked with the natural development of music notations. One wonders how they ever became separated in the traditional teaching practice where notation and music theory are taught in the absence of an instrument. Again, this notion will be expanded on in later chapters. At this point, however, what is critical for teachers to realize is that children will invent music notations as they are exploring instruments and creating compositions. In a remarkable study by Borstad (1989, 1990), the author relates how Grade 1 children systematically created meaningful music notations for pieces they had composed on simple "sound-makers"—terra cotta garden pots, bells, drums, whistles, copper piping, and the like (see Figure 1–2). Borstad's work is exciting not only because of the intriguing notations developed by the children in a learner-directed environment, but because *the classroom teacher had no formal musical training*, yet was able to set the conditions to make it possible for children to create and develop music notations of their own.

I could list even more conditions or features of classrooms which would enhance the development of children's notations. In the chapters which follow, those that have already been described are developed, and others are considered. For now, however, only the flavor of those conditions needs to be sampled, with the understanding that creating an environment where children are free to mess around with instruments, and where their compositions and notations will be appreciated, honored, and developed, is decidedly more important than teaching notation explicitly. In fact, I cannot imagine the learning of music notation occurring unless children can create their own meaning and work. The difficulty, of course, is putting that philosophy to the test. In so doing, one must trust the children enough to believe that they will create meaningful patterns of music notation, with some thoughtful interventions on the part of their teachers to extend the directions that they take in their work.

Even if one is convinced that children might be able to develop their own music notation systems, one also needs to understand that one can make sense of children's music notations, even if one cannot read standard music notation. As adults, we have had much experience in decoding various kinds of symbol systems, and

FIGURE 1–2 *A piece written by a Grade 1 student for two sets of hand bells and whistle (from J. Borstad 1990.* But I've been pouring sounds all day. *Unpublished Master's thesis, Queen's University, Kingston, Ontario.)*

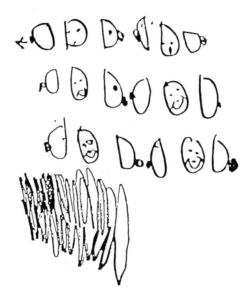

The circles are all pictures of the child's face, either in profile (nose showing) or facing the front. When the child drew herself facing left, she played the bells on her left hand, and when facing right, the bells on her right hand. When she was facing forward, she blew the whistle. The pattern of left shake, whistle, right shake was repeated six times without variation, and then the piece ended (jiggly lines) by all three instruments playing together.

music notation is nothing more than another such system. Obviously, we are fluent with text, and with symbols of arithmetic. We read books and newspapers, we calculate unit prices at the grocery store, we (sometimes) balance checkbooks. We also deal with pictures or iconic symbols—icons indicating men's and women's washrooms, departing and arriving airplanes, traffic signs, and the like. All of these systems carry meaning, and by interpreting these symbols, we make choices and take actions. Music notations are no different. In fact, since children often borrow from other symbol systems in creating their own music notations, many of the symbols they use are familiar to us, even if they are used in unfamiliar ways. For instance, children will use letters, words, and numbers in their music notations. Just like the other symbols we interpret, some are relatively straightforward (like familiar icons for men's and women's washrooms) while others may cause some confusion (I once followed what I thought was a symbol for baggage pick-up at a European airport, only to find myself facing rows and rows of lockers). Some examples and descriptions of children's invented notations follow, both of the "washrooms" and "baggage pick-up" variety.

The notation in Figure 1–3 was produced by two seven-year-old children. One child ("C") played the wood block, and the other ("D") played the tambourine. The first line (C C D D 2x) was played with one instrument at a time (two taps on the wood block, two taps on the tambourine; repeated). The next two lines were performed with both instruments playing at once. The last line, with the alternating C D pattern, was again performed with the two instruments playing separately. As one can readily imagine, the "2x" notation means "play the line two times." (Since rhythm patterns often have repetitions, it is very common for children to use the symbol "2x" to indicate that a pattern is to be played two times, borrowing from their knowledge of mathematical symbols.) The middle section was played faster than the others. This, however, is not evident from the notation.

Quite a different notation is given in Figure 1–4. This notation can be viewed as instrument dependent, that is, the particular system chosen by the child was influenced by the instrument on which the piece was composed. In this case, an eight-year-old child had written a piece for a xylophone, and the letter names for the pitches were engraved on each note of the instrument. To make further distinctions between different notes of the same name, the child has used "L" to indicate low notes, and correspondingly, "h" to indicate high notes, and provided a legend indicating the same. Notice that the "2x" symbol appears again, except this time, the "2x" refers not to the entire line, but only to the last note of the line. This is impossible to tell from the notation, but in listening to the child play the piece, the use of the "2x" symbol becomes clear. Similarly, some of the notes were played more quickly than others, but again, this could only be determined from the child's performance of the piece, not from the notation. Children rarely notate all features of their melodies, rather, they notate those as-

FIGURE 1-3 *Piece for wood block and tambourine*

The child's invented notation, using letters and numbers and other symbols:

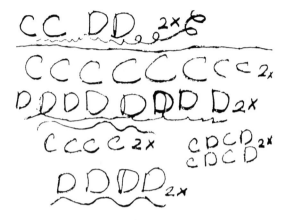

The piece as it would appear in standard notation:

4/4 wood block			
tambourine			

(standard music notation for wood block and tambourine)

FIGURE 1–4 *Piece for xylophone*
(This figure appears in *This Too Is Music*: Upitis 1990b, p. 70.)

The child's invented notation, differentiating the same notes at two different octaves, using L (low) and h (high):

The piece as it would appear in standard notation:

pects of the **melody** that to them are most salient—in this case, **pitch**.

The next example of a child's notation shown in Figure 1–5 is a piece written for four glass bottles, filled with water at various levels. It is not possible to tell what the pitches for each of the bottles were from the notation, and in fact, the pitches didn't seem to matter much to the child, for when asked, she commented, "Well, as long as you can tell they're different, it's O.K." As this ten-year-old child was creating her notation, she was very aware of the fact that the notation might be read by someone else, and wanted to be sure that her intentions were clear. Several times over the course of the twenty minutes that she spent writing this piece, she called me over and explained her symbols, even though her notation was quite simple to read.

The notation in Figure 1–6 is one eight-year-old child's way of notating a familiar song, *Twinkle, Twinkle, Little Star*. I am particularly fond of this notation, since the notation successfully captures phrases or chunks of the melody, and outlines the general shape of the melody in a highly visual way. This child has even managed to indicate that the melody ends the way it begins, by drawing the arrow back to the beginning, and closing the piece with a bracket. (In fact, the arrow drawn by the child is not quite accurate. The dotted line indicates where the arrowhead should have been placed.) Although some people, both those with and without music reading background, have trouble reading this notation, once the pitch and phrasing system used by the child is understood, the notation becomes quite clear (see Figure 1–6 for more detail).

The examples of children's notations contained in Figures 1–3 through 1–6 present little challenge in interpretation, since they are strongly tied to simple instruments, or, in the case of *Twinkle, Twinkle, Little Star*, the notation represents a familiar song. Some notations are more challenging. One needs to bear in mind, however, that these notations need not be interpreted in the dark. Just as a teacher will often ask a child to read his or her story, so too should the teacher ask the child to play his or her song. In the playing of the song, the way that the notation hangs together often becomes clear. This is a process that never ends. Even though I

FIGURE 1–5 *Piece for four glass bottles*

Composing a Piece for Xylophone Using Letter Names for Pitch

have read many thousands of notations, and in so doing, learned how to read a great variety of invented notations, I still encounter the odd notation that causes me some confusion. In these puzzling cases, it is particularly important to ask the child to explain the system. In any case, while we never have the time to hear every piece or hear every story, asking children to routinely play their songs gives them the message that their work is important, and that we are trying to make meaning from their work as well.

Having made the claim that one can, with the help of the children involved, learn to read children's notations of music, I would like to make a further argument supporting the importance of allowing children to develop their own notational systems. All too often, the formal or standardized system is taught first, with little attention to children's natural development in understanding the system in question. Bamberger and Schön (1980) convincingly argue that in order to understand formal symbol systems, individuals must first construct their own versions of symbol systems. By

FIGURE I-6 *A child's notation for* Twinkle, Twinkle, Little Star

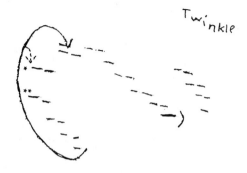

The notation begins at the asterisk (*), and is read from left to right. Part of the notation is read twice, so the reader is expected to ignore the bracket the first time through. At the end of the first line, the notation continues at the double asterisk (**). The reader is then told to loop back to the beginning, as indicated by the arrow. As noted previously, the arrowhead should actually appear as indicated by the dotted line, rather than where the child has drawn the arrow. This second time, reading again left to right, the piece ends at the bracket.

Twinkle, Twinkle, Little Star as it appears in standard notation:

formal, Bamberger and Schön refer to systems where some fixed-reference and symbol system can be used to describe a series of related objects or events. For example, using a map drawn on a grid system with North-South-East-West referents would be a formal system for describing the path from *A* to *B*. On the other hand, telling about the path from *A* to *B* using descriptions that are not standardized or fixed in terms of direction or measurement of distance (e.g., "Go for a few minutes on the gravel road, and then turn right by the big tree.") would be described as figural by Bamberger and Schön. These two types of systems are qualitatively different, and the symbol systems generated by each point of view differ accordingly. Many children use figural descriptions to notate their music, while standard music notation, with its fixed referents in terms of durations and tonality, is a formal system. Historically, in music notation and in other areas as well (e.g., geometry), figural systems were created first. It is therefore not surprising that children would create symbol systems of a figural nature as well. Some of the fascinating parallels between children's development of music notation and the historical development of Western music notation are touched on again in later chapters.

One can easily acknowledge the importance of allowing **figural notations** to develop, rather than beginning with the presentation of formal knowledge systems. But it is also true that in order to make the links to formal, standardized notation, one needs to be able to read and use standard notation. Although a teacher may not need to read standard notation to begin encouraging and promoting composition by his or her students, there comes a point where it makes sense to learn about standard notation, in order to help develop children's notations to a greater degree. So, we have now reached the biggest hurdle—the one that this chapter is all about.

I'd like to make the rather bold statement that reading standard music notation, at an elementary level at least, is really not that hard. So much of the mystery that surrounds music-making seems to be shrouded in this business of standard notation, and yet, once the cover is removed, what lies underneath is rather simple. By now, I have asked you to make sense of several notations of children, and my guess is that you have found them meaningful, and interesting to interpret. It might be encouraging to realize that many children's notations are in fact far *more* complex than standard notation. Often when children fashion a notational system and develop it, the system becomes so cumbersome that it is very difficult to read (see Figure 1–7). When this happens, standard notation is a welcome relief to both students and myself. I recall well a comment from the child who produced the notation in Figure 1–7, when I showed him his song in standard notation. He embraced the system, realizing its elegance after grappling with his own, and exclaimed, "I wonder who thought *that* one up!"

I now invite you to take a look at Figure 1–8. It is a common

FIGURE 1–7 *A complex invented notation*
(This figure appears in *This Too Is Music*: Upitis 1990b, p. 67.)

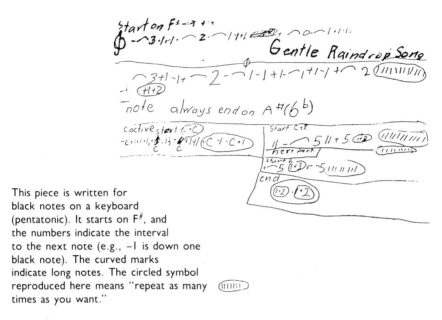

This piece is written for black notes on a keyboard (pentatonic). It starts on F#, and the numbers indicate the interval to the next note (e.g., –1 is down one black note). The curved marks indicate long notes. The circled symbol reproduced here means "repeat as many times as you want."

The piece as it would appear in standard notation:

FIGURE 1-8 *Standard notation of a familiar children's melody*

children's tune, written in standard notation. In order to make sense of it, try humming it, either in your head, or better yet, out loud. Or at least, try tapping the rhythm—notes that look the same have the same **duration**. I am sure the tune will be recognized even by those readers who claim that they don't know how to read music. As you look at it, try and figure out why some notes are filled, why some are hollow. What does the double vertical line indicate at the end? How are high notes shown? How does this notation parallel the child's notation shown in Figure 1–6 for *Twinkle, Twinkle, Little Star*?

I expect that some of you were grinning when you recognized the tune. Too easy? Try making sense of the melodies in Figure 1–9. Why are some of the stems joined? What does the double number at the beginning indicate? What is the point of having a **treble clef** at the beginning of each line?

If you haven't deciphered the notations, don't turn to the back of the book looking for the answers! Just as children grapple with reading the notations of others, both standard and invented, I am sure that all of us learn best by trying to figure things out on our own, and when we choose, with the help of others. So, if you are still unsure about the identity of some of the songs in Figure 1–9, ask someone. The person you ask need not be a musician, or even an adult. I have seen many children figure out different aspects of notations, both of their own invention and of the standard format, by puzzling over them for a few minutes together.

I cannot emphasize enough that learning to read is an ongoing process. Whether we are reading text, interpreting mathematical symbols and relationships, or reading music, it is always possible to reach higher levels of fluency and sophistication. Even musicians who have been reading standard notation for many years find

FIGURE 1-9 *Further standard notation examples of children's melodies*

themselves having to learn to read new systems. For example, a great deal of twentieth century music is notated in new standard forms, due to the emergence of new musical forms and instruments, particularly those associated with electronic and computer-driven systems (see Figure 1–10). Musicians who had been reading what we usually refer to as standard notation often resisted learning these new forms. But people *do* learn new forms of notation, especially if these notations make sense in the context of the music they are writing or performing, despite that all too familiar wave of initial resistance. I know it myself. While I have yet to learn to read some of the notations developed in the past few decades, in the past year I have had to grapple with learning to read the **tenor clef** in learning to play the 'cello. As a pianist, I can read treble and **bass clefs** fluently, but reading the tenor clef, where all of the notes fall on different lines and spaces, is another matter. I remember asking my teacher, "Do I really have to learn to read tenor clef?", sounding just like a timorous eight-year-old piano student

FIGURE 1-10 *Examples of 20th century "new standard" notations*
(from R. Rastall 1982. *The notation of Western music.* New York:
St. Martin's Press.)

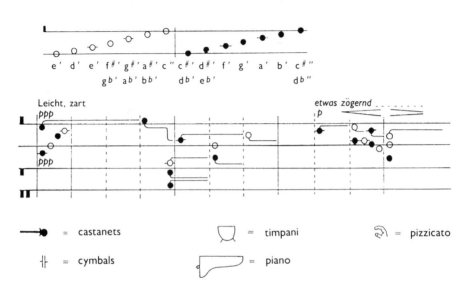

confronted with having to learn to read treble and bass clefs. As
soon as the words were out of my mouth, we both laughed. I
realized that I already had the advantage of reading other clefs,
and if I could do it as a child, surely, I could learn as an adult—
an adult who spends a good amount of her time researching and
writing about notational forms. And of course, once I decided to
do it, learning to read the tenor clef certainly wasn't nearly as
difficult as I had feared.

And now, a final observation. Most of this chapter was written
on a hot and sunny day in late August. I was working at a computer, overlooking a pond from a large log house in the middle of
a forest. There were four or five children of various ages playing
in and around the pond, and on the verandah below. As I was
working, I overheard many interactions between the children and
their mothers, while keeping an ear and an eye open for my own.
At one point, the youngest, a three-year-old, asked for pen and
paper, and proceeded to draw a picture of a person (see Figure

FIGURE 1–11 *Jesse's person*

1–11). Later, when I went downstairs for a cup of tea, I saw the drawing on the table. Jessica's mother, who has six older children as well, casually commented, "Oh look! She's started drawing legs. And see, she can do the eyes, nose, mouth, and ears now. Sometimes she does cheeks too. Pretty soon we'll get the feet, and then the arms, and fingers." I laughingly agreed, commenting on how common it was for children to develop their drawings of people in this way.

Children's notations of music are just as predictable, I thought to myself, as is their development of writing, their understanding of mathematical concepts, and so on. I carried the cup of tea upstairs, freshly enthused about writing this book. In the pages that follow, I will relate, through stories and examples, how we can recognize and encourage children's notations of music. In so doing, I hope that you find their work as funny, magical, clever, ingenious, and precious as do I, and find ways to make this kind of work possible in their everyday lives.

Creating a Rich Music Setting

▲ ▲ ▲ ▲ ▲ ▲ ▲ ▲ ▲ ▲ ▲ ▲ ▲ ▲ ▲ ▲ ▲ ▲   ALTHOUGH I made references in the first chapter to classrooms, the nurturing of children's notational development need by no means be limited to classroom environments. Indeed, the examples that are given throughout this book were collected from a great variety of settings—homes of friends and colleagues, children's music lessons outside of school, small groups in school settings, intact classroom settings, camps— in almost any situation where children's music-making might occur.

These settings varied in a number of ways. Some were very private—a piece composed and notated by a child and shared only at a music lesson, or only with a parent. Some were the opposite— many notations described in this book were developed by an entire class involved in improvisation, composition, and notation. Others fell somewhere in between—small groups of children writing music in semiformal instructional settings.

The situations also varied in terms of how the children interacted with adults. Often the adult, either a teacher, parent, or family friend, was involved in a way that might seem only incidental—as someone who happened to be nearby when an audience was needed. Sometimes an adult played a more direct role, offering encouragement or technical advice as the child was creating. There were times as well when an adult set a specific task, asking all children to participate in some way.

Regardless of the situations in which the compositions described herein were created, it will be seen that the range of instrumentation used by the children and the sophistication of the children as composers varied tremendously. Within this variation, however, patterns of notational development emerge. These will be discussed in detail in the next chapter.

One might well ask what these various situations have in common, and how a rich music setting might be characterized to include all of the possibilities just listed. In the previous chapter, I described some of the features of classrooms and characteristics of teachers that I considered important for nurturing children's abilities to read and write music notations. These features included honoring the directions taken by the learner, providing materials for exploration, acknowledging the meaning in children's work, and encouraging the development of notational systems in the context of real music-making. All of these conditions are important, in fact, critical, if children are to develop as composers, whether that development takes place in a classroom, at home, or through private music lessons.

Of course, even if the conditions as those described above are provided, one cannot expect that this will effortlessly and automatically lead to a generation of prolific child composers. As those who have been encouraging "whole language" for the past decade will attest, merely listing conditions will do little to effect change, even in the most willing teachers. These things have to be practiced, internalized, and seen as integral to a philosophy of music teaching before any serious change can occur. Such internalization takes time, and support in many forms—from colleagues, administrators, in-service leaders, parents, and most important of all, the children themselves. Teachers who have embraced the intent of the whole language approach have a great advantage in attempting to encourage music composition and notation through the same process, for many of the essential practices in both domains overlap. I might also add that parents have always been whole language teachers, for their natural instincts in teaching children to speak and helping them begin to write and read mirror the whole language approaches now embraced by teachers in developing children's writing.

With the preceding *caveat*, I now turn to what I consider the features that rich music settings have in common. These features can be seen as overlapping in many ways, and are by no means inclusive of all possibilities. It is my experience, however, that if these conditions prevail, many interesting discoveries will be made by children and their teachers as they create and perform music for each other.

Setting the Scene

Surround Children with Music Symbols and Sound

Children of our culture are aware of print from an early age. They cannot help but see it in many forms—road signs, newspapers, books, magazines, advertising signs, and the print on cereal boxes and jam jars. I should think that it would be a rare day when a child did not somehow encounter print, and moreover, see people using print. It may not be clear to them for some years just what kind of meaning print carries, but they know two things: print is everywhere, and print means something. They see adults and older siblings make sense of print every day—reading books and newspapers, following recipes, and reading road signs. In addition to these casual encounters with print, many children are read to, are taught the alphabet song, and in numerous other ways, sensitized to the existence of letters and words. It is a small wonder that they soon begin scribbling, and then forming letters—the letters of their names, the other letters of the alphabet, along with other writing scribbles (see Figure 1–1 in the previous chapter). This development is fostered, as most parents encourage the process of becoming familiar with print, taking delight in seeing their children beginning to form recognizable letters. While parents often realize that the child may not be, say, associating a sound with a letter or imagining the letter as part of a word, it is enough that they are experimenting with the elements of the printed word.

Unfortunately, there is no parallel for the symbols of music. Is it possible that one of the reasons that few children naturally write music is that they are not sensitized to the symbols of music, and to the fact that such symbols have meaning? While a few children may see music notation if their parents or older siblings read notation to play an instrument, most children have very little exposure to the symbols of music, even on television. In schools, there is also comparatively little in the way of music notation in evidence. Even in music classrooms, there are more often pictures of instruments than examples of notation—partly, I suspect, because of the misguided notion that there is little point displaying music scores that the children don't (yet) understand. But I am convinced that it is precisely this lack of exposure to music notations—of any form—that makes it difficult to realize how music symbols are related to sound, that they have meaning, and that they can be used to communicate and create. No one expects a two-year-old to understand the complex relationship between print and meaning, but that doesn't stop parents from reading stories, following the words with a finger, and generally sharing the impact of print with their child. I have a friend who started reading *The Cremation of Sam McGee* to his child when he was eighteen months. He read it to Graeme because he was thrilled with the meter and rhyme of the poem, the humor of it, and the fine illustrations in the book. Of course he knew that his son couldn't understand the words and meanings. But he also knew that this book was a great source of delight for them both. Just because print—or notation—is too complex, doesn't mean that it shouldn't be shared with children.

In the previous chapter, an example of a music scribble was shown (see Figure 1–1). This scribble was produced by a child who was literally surrounded by music—a variety of music to listen to, instruments to play, and music scores to look at. The role of music notation was clear to him from an early age. Once, when his mother was commenting that she wished she could play a Chopin Nocturne that she had just listened to on the radio, Joel looked at her with his incredulous five-year-old eyes and asked her why she didn't go to the store to buy the right book. (Surely with the right book in front of her at the piano, the right sounds would emerge from her fingers.)

When children are surrounded by the symbols of music, it is not at all surprising to see them playing with those symbols in the same way that they scribble and form letters. Just as a child makes strings of letters that don't form words, the child who plays with music symbols creates combinations that don't make melodies (see Figure 2–1). But in both cases, the child is making an attempt at understanding the meaning behind these symbols, playing with their power. As Wells (1986) so aptly argues, children are meaning

FIGURE 2–1 *Early use of symbols*

Music

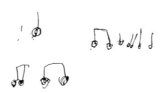

Letters

makers from the start, and each move that they make should be recognized and explored as an attempt at meaning making. In this way, Wells argues that much can be achieved in extending their ways of making sense of language, text, and the world at large.

I would like to go back for a moment to look at the two sets of symbols in Figure 2–1 in some detail. The strings of letters shown in Figure 2–1 are identified by Gentry (1982) as belonging to what he terms the "precommunicative" stage of spelling. He argues that this is the very earliest level of spelling development, which occurs after children have been engaged in the writing activity of handling a pen or pencil to make scribbles. At this precommunicative stage, children often use single letters of the alphabet to represent entire words. In so doing, the children demonstrate that they have some knowledge of the alphabet. Nevertheless, they have no knowledge of letter-sound correspondence. Further, children, at this stage, may or may not understand that the text of our culture is read from left to right. Gentry has observed that children also mix in numbers at this precommunicative stage of spelling, and that upper and lowercase letters are used indiscriminately with the children often having a preference for uppercase letters. (I wonder if children see more uppercase letters?)

I am sure that there is a direct parallel here between a child's attempts at spelling and a child's attempts at writing music. I would hesitate to use the term precommunicative, since there is considerable communication taking place when the child offers this kind of artifact to a parent or teacher. The use of music symbols shown in Figure 2–1 can nevertheless be described by the same characteristics. The child demonstrates some knowledge of standard music symbols, and realizes that they are used to represent meaning. But the child does not understand how a given symbol represents pitch or duration. As with the precommunicative stage of spelling, the child may well use a music symbol to represent an entire piece of music. Further, the child may or may not understand that music also has left-right directionality, and may include other symbols as well. In addition to music symbols, a child who is playing with symbols may make drawings, letters, and numbers to accompany the symbols of music (see Figure 2–2). Just as a precommunicative speller mixes upper- and lowercase letters, a child playing with the symbols of music mixes symbols of various types of meanings (different durations, clefs). For all of these reasons, it is perhaps best to think of this stage of development in understanding stan-

---

FIGURE 2–2 *Mixing music symbols with other symbols*

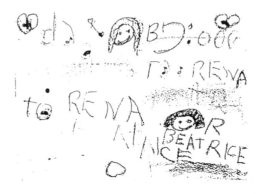

Here the child is mixing music symbols with all kinds of other things—words, pictures, and icons—and adding stickers with similar symbols and color in creating the whole "picture".

---

dard music notation as the first of a series of meaningful attempts to use symbols of music—an "early" rather than "pre" communicative stage.

Further parallels between the natural development of standardized spelling and the development of the use of standard notation are pursued throughout this book. While all of the spelling stages cannot be as neatly mapped onto the development of understanding of music notation as can this first stage, there are some compelling similarities, and correspondingly, parallel implications for teaching and learning. For now, however, I would like to turn to another way that children can be surrounded by music, and that is by sound itself.

The notion of enriching the sounds that children hear is simply an extension of the idea just described, namely exposing children to examples of musical text. For children are not only surrounded by print, they are surrounded by spoken language. Similarly, if it makes sense to surround children with the symbols of music, then it certainly makes sense to surround them with the sounds. In fact, were this not a book on music notation, I would probably have written about sound first. But of course, the two are naturally intertwined—symbol and sound are hardly separate from each other.

Some children are fortunate in that they hear music from a variety of sources, but again, there is much more that can be done in this regard—at home, at school, and at private music lessons. The music we know best is the most accessible, and it is easy to fall into the trap of listening to what we know. I find myself continually trying to listen to and learn about new music, that is, music that is new to me. In so doing, I am also able to provide new music for the children that I teach. But it is hard. I am aware that while I provide my students with a broad variety of Baroque, Classical, Romantic, and to a somewhat lesser extent, Folk music (from North America and from my own Latvian heritage), it is more difficult to make other less familiar music available to them—music from South America, music by early twentieth century American composers, and the music of the Native people of our own country, to name but a few. But I continue to try. Not only is my own musical diet more varied as a result, but also I am sure that by providing children with the experience of hearing music from various periods and cultures, I do them a double service. First, it gives them the opportunity to make their musical palettes more rich. Second, it shows that a huge variety of sounds, textures, and pat-

Playing Around on an Instrument at Home

terns combine to form the music of our world. This can only make children's own compositions more interesting. And so, their notations become more diverse as well.

Provide a Variety of Instruments To Play

Of course children need to do more than see and hear music. It almost goes without saying that children need to experiment with sound to improvise, compose, and develop notational systems. But again, this is a circumstance which occurs too rarely. While one sees many common rhythm instruments—drums, tambourines, shakers, bells—in the homes of toddlers, at day cares, and in kindergartens, it seems that those instruments virtually disappear as children reach the early primary grades. It is not that the instruments are not available, in the schools, but that they are hidden from sight. When they are brought out from storage, they are usually used in a manner prescribed by a teacher. Using instruments in ordered ways is not a bad thing, of course. The problem comes when children no longer have the opportunity to play freely with the instruments. There will be more said about the interplay between outside structure and child-directed play later in the book. For now, suffice it to say that one form of using instruments should never be to the exclusion of the other.

It is also true that the simple rhythm instruments sometimes lose their appeal as children get older. Somehow the red plastic tambourine that was used by a child at the age of three doesn't seem quite as attractive when the child is eight. The problem, as I see it, is that we fail to provide an ever increasing set of new, and possibly more sophisticated, instruments for children to learn to play, or just to play around with. In many homes, once the "red toy tambourine stage" is over, the only instruments to be found are those that the children are learning to play through private lessons, or with a school band. This is changing somewhat with new technology; with the decreasing prices of synthesizer keyboards, more parents are purchasing such instruments for the home—sometimes as a toy. But there are so many more possibilities, which I am only beginning to take advantage of myself.

I have had the good fortune to travel a great deal, but it took me some time to get into the habit of bringing home an instrument from the places I had visited and even lived. There was a long period during which I felt that if I didn't know how to play an instrument then that instrument didn't have a legitimate place in my home. (After all, what if someone asked me to play one of my instruments, and I didn't know how?) Thus, I had, for example, soprano and tenor recorders, both of which I could play, but not an alto recorder, which I did not play. Somewhere along the way, I brought home an instrument that I didn't know how to play. Now I am happy to collect instruments whenever and however I can find them. As a result, I have a great number of interesting rhythm instruments—from Kenya, from Sierra Leone, from Bali, from the Caribbean. But I also have wind instruments that I cannot play (but I can play with), and others that I am learning to play. In this process, I have also begun to collect things that make nice sounds—instruments that are not conventional, but by that are no less appropriate for creating musical sounds. And so, I collect things like leftover bits of copper pipe (to blow or to strike), and sticks and bottles that make fine sounds. Even the red plastic tambourine becomes, once again, a "good" instrument in this collection. And ultimately, the real beauty of having this smorgasbord of instruments is that people gravitate towards them and start to play. Experimentation on one instrument soon leads to experimentation on another. If there are several people in the house, it is almost laughably predictable to see a little ensemble strike up. This kind of experimentation and play does not occur only with trained musicians. There is something purely inviting about seeing instruments that are obviously meant to be played.

Treat Children as Composers

Children readily beat away at the drums and shake the tambourines they are given as youngsters, becoming instant performers. But it can also take surprisingly little time for a child to begin to see himself or herself as a composer. In fact, often the younger the children, the easier it is for them to get into the act of composing—probably because they haven't yet learned that composing is something reserved for a few elite people (probably dead, European, and male, with family names like Beethoven, Bach, or Mozart). But even older children, who may initially treat composition as a special undertaking, can quickly shake off their hesitations if the circumstances are right.

I often begin with a very simple activity—one that works with children as young as four, as well as with adult students and practicing classroom teachers. The activity is this: I ask the children (or adults) to find a partner, and for each person to pick an instrument, usually a simple rhythm instrument such as a drum or a tambourine, or a pitched instrument like a recorder. I then ask the pair to "make up a song" using the two instruments, and then to "write something down so that someone else in the room can play it." I am convinced that it is important to give no further instructions, tempted though one might be to talk about the kinds of symbols that might be used, or the length of the piece, or thinking about how the two instruments might be combined. When I have not resisted the temptation to help, I have found that children's creations are less interesting—they tend to treat my suggestions as the right way to do this task, and are also more critical of their work, expecting more of themselves than I would. Another reason for keeping it simple is that when one is on tender ground, especially with adults who might have a hard time thinking of themselves as composers, it is probably best to make light of the activity, rather than weighing it down with unnecessary parame-

Working with a Partner on a Composition

ters. Finally, by giving such simple instructions, and then giving the children or adults a good deal of time to get on with the task (anywhere from forty minutes to two hours), it helps to establish the expectation that this is something that I not only expect they can do without much guidance from me, but something they can be actively engaged in for quite some time—just like a young child playing with an instrument might do if granted with the gift of some uninterrupted time.

Recall that I also suggested that children or adults should work in pairs for this activity. One reason for this is that it relieves the pressure of coming up with something spectacular on a solo venture. But another, and perhaps more important reason in the long run, is that I firmly believe that one learns more through social interaction than in solitary reflection, especially when an activity is relatively new and exploratory. The potential for creating notations and learning about symbol systems is further enhanced when children trade notations with each other, something I touch on in the next section, and explore in depth in Chapter 5.

Before I continue, however, I cannot state strongly enough that if one believes children can compose, children will come to believe that they can compose, and do so. This is probably true of any endeavor that requires one to see oneself in a new way. In another context, I wrote about my early endeavors as a beginning adult 'cellist, and how important it was for me to regard myself as a 'cellist from the very beginning, in fact from the first lesson (Upitis 1990b). I have progressed quickly since then, partly because I have had the benefit of many years of playing the piano, but more so, I am sure, because I believed I was a 'cellist right from the squeaky start. I have been helped in that belief by my teacher. After I had been taking lessons for about six months, my teacher quietly mentioned one day that I could be playing some of the simple movements from the Bach 'cello suites in a few months' time. I was astounded at his projection, and vowed to practice enough so that his prediction would be borne out. Well, a few months later I had indeed managed one of the **Minuets** from the first **Suite**. So, my teacher was right. But I wonder if I would have progressed as quickly had he not broached the possibility, and in so doing, demonstrated his faith in my future ability.

Generate a Real Need for Notation

By asking children to "make up a song" and then "write something down so that someone else can play it," one is both requiring that a notation be created and implying that children are capable of producing such a notation. After a group of children have done this, I usually ask them to trade notations with someone else, and then try to read each other's notations on each other's instruments. The outcome of doing this can both be funny and instructive. Faced with someone else's interpretation of one's own notation, children are, more often than not, gleefully surprised by the results. But this is, in some ways, a contrived way of having children begin to generate notations. There is really no *need* for a child to notate his or her composition when someone in the same room will be reading it. As children have often pointed out to me, "I don't need to write it down. I can just show him."

It takes very little, however, for a real need to emerge. Recently, after having had children compose in the manner I have described for some weeks, two girls composed a melody for a poem. They were uncontainably proud of their work. It wasn't enough to share it with the members of the class—they wanted the whole school to have a copy of their song. At this point the issues around notation became critical for them. For several days, I heard conversations about how they could notate the song so that the school secretary could read their notation, transcribe it on the computer, and publish it for the whole school. This real need for notation arises when a composer wants to share a work with others, others that he or she will not meet directly, but who will be faced with a piece of music which hopefully captures the composer's intent.

There is a parallel in the historical development of notation here as well. People did not always notate everything they composed and played. One of the first standard forms of notation evolved for the Gregorian Chant, part of the sacred music of the churches. There was, however, no such notation for secular music—music outside the church. But when the secular musicians began to travel in the latter part of the Middle Ages, these musicians and composers developed a standard form of music notation (Grout 1960). What had begun as an oral tradition, where well known melodic formulas were applied to a given text, became a written tradition when the repertoire of the melodies grew increasingly complex and numerous. Consequently, a more precise form of notation was developed. By the twelfth and thirteenth centuries, the troubadours, traveling poets, and composers, were notating compositions in standardized ways. These compositions were copied into song collections for the traveling artists to use and share. From this evolved the familiar standard notation of this century, a notation that is still evolving. In this way, personal history mirrors cultural history—children's notations develop as they need to notate either more complex melodies or share their notations with others.

I would like to close this section with yet another observation that relates to the premise that it only makes sense to teach about notation when there is a need for notation. I often encounter the argument that not everyone needs notation. I have even made that argument myself sometimes when I have encountered teachers who are so concerned about teaching music notation that they seem to be forgetting the music-making itself. But while it is true that blind musicians manage without notation, and that many folk guitar players learn extremely well through imitation and by ear, it is also true that understanding something about a notational system can be a useful thing. One doesn't have to use a notational system to function as a musician. But being unable to use notation means that some dimension of music cannot be readily accessed. I often wonder what people miss by not reading music, since I have read music nearly all of my life, and cannot imagine what it would be like not to read music. It is a bit like imagining what it must be like to be illiterate in terms of print—how can those of us who read with ease imagine what it is like not to be able to make sense of the words on this page? We cannot imagine it, but we know that we would like others to share our knowledge, and the worlds that such knowledge opens.

Children need a notation system of some sort when they become composers, an extension of exploring the sounds that an instrument can make. The notations of children, as I have already illustrated, certainly need not be standard, at least at the outset, but they must be systematic. In this way, children can use their notations to preserve their works, to re-create them at a later date, to modify and elaborate their works, and to share their works with others. Children have all of these needs when they are composers, and notation serves as a tool to meet those needs.

Provide Serious Feedback
About Children's Compositions

If children are using notation in the context of composition, it is important to work with those notations, extending the meaning that the children are making through their use of symbols in the way that Wells (1986) talks about extending language through conversation. While it is important to praise the achievements of children as their compositions develop, it is equally important to provide useful and critical feedback about their work. In doing so, we give children the message that we believe their work is important enough to treat seriously, to criticize, to modify, to rework, to share again. Some compositions are simply not as successful as others, and children know this as well as the adults who teach them. Just as some paintings or stories show more imagination than others, so too do the musical creations of children. It would be a mistake to treat all compositions in the same way, and this is apparent to children as well as to the adults with whom they may share their works.

I remember well an incident with a child a few months ago. He had written several pieces to which I gave little attention, other than to encourage him to continue the process. At one point, however, he came up with a piece for chimes that I found quite lovely.

I spent a chunk of class time with him—10 or 15 minutes—launching into questions about his choices of rhythms and symbols, and making criticisms and suggestions about what he might repeat and change. I doubt whether I ever explicitly stated that I liked the piece. But he knew I did, for I overheard him say to another child a few minutes later, "Miss Upitis *really* liked this one!" There is perhaps no better way to tell a child that we think his or her work is important and good than to invest time in developing and extending the work.

Create a Community of Musicians

One of the reasons that the composition activity described earlier in this chapter works well is that it is embedded in a context where all the children together form a community of composers. I have written at length about the importance of establishing such a community in another book, and ways in which this can occur (Upitis 1990b). What follows is a summary of what I view as the main elements of a successful music community.

Perhaps the most important thing to create for children is a way of seeing themselves in relation to other performers and composers. This happens as soon as children are engaged in the act of composition. It matters not that they might be using different instruments, and creating wildly divergent works. What matters

Children Improvising a Recorder and Piano Duet

is that they are absorbed by the same enterprise. They can ask each other questions, share discoveries, play for each other. They can read each other's notations. In this way, the sharing of works is an integral part of the music experience. This kind of sharing and performance can, and should, occur on a very local level—just playing a piece for a couple of kids that happen to be nearby, or for the class sometime during the period, is a way of sharing that can occur immediately and should never stop. This is very much like sharing stories or journal entries children have written. While a child is unlikely to read every story or every journal entry to the class, a few are certainly worth making public. Of course, when all of the children are involved in the same process, they are both an informed and critical audience. Just like the child who knew I liked his piece because I was critical of it, so too do children realize that sharing a work for the purpose of critical comment is to validate the work, not the opposite.

Another kind of performance is important as well. When I spent a year as a full-time music teacher in an inner-city school in Boston, one of the regular events was the "Thursday Recess Concert." There, children could perform their own works, and works of other composers (some of the dead, European, and male variety). They performed both as soloists and as members of ensembles. The Recess Concerts were an important aspect in developing a strong music community, for not only did children have the opportunity to see their own works performed in a slightly more formal setting, but their works were performed alongside those of other composers—Pergolesi, Mozart, and Barber. When children have had such regular opportunities to perform and to listen, there is a broad base for launching larger productions as well. But whether large productions are part of the picture or not, the important thing to provide is a way for children's works to be noticed, criticized, extended, and celebrated, not in a way that is separate from the processes of composition and notation, but in a way that is embodied in those acts.

Modifying Existing Settings

Home

I have a new neighbor. Living in the country, as I do, one tends to spend a good deal of time with one's neighbors. Relationships with neighbors are not to be taken lightly. They are a crucial part

Performing a Piece for Saxophone and Piano

of the community we all enjoy, depend on, and thrive on. Belonging in a community of country dwellers is not unlike belonging
to a community of musicians such as the one described above.

During one of our first getting acquainted conversations, our
talk predictably settled on the topic of work. "How," asked David,
"do you spend your time?" It's always a bit of a struggle for me
to answer this question. I could go on for hours about children's
notations (and sometimes I do), but that's not necessarily the best
way to begin a neighborly chat. Often it's better to talk about corn
and tomatoes. But—it wasn't a corn and tomatoes day. And so, I
picked a few careful phrases, outlining the skeleton of all of this—
telling him that I am a musician, that I teach both at a public school
and at the university, and that I have private students as well. I
went on to say that besides being interested in teaching and performance, I was attempting to uncover some of the ways that
children notate music, particularly as they compose their own
music.

I expected our conversation to end politely at that point.
Enough information had been given, and I was happy to have
wormed in a sentence or two about this notation business. I was
pleasantly surprised to find that he wanted to hear more. A fellow

musician, I thought. But no, just a parent of two teenaged children, both of whom had spent time in private music lessons, and abandoned their instruments in the end—an unfortunate but common lament. David's interest in this work was that it made intuitive sense to him—learning music and music notation through creation rather than solely through performance.

We talked for a good part of the afternoon. What I remember the most from that conversation was his dismay that he "couldn't imagine noticing" if one of his children, as a preschooler, had offered the kinds of musical scribbles described earlier. He further observed that they probably wouldn't have created notations at home unless they *needed* to write something down, and expected one of their parents to share in the communication. As our conversation progressed, he outlined many possibilities for modifying the home experience so that this kind of natural music making and writing might occur. Many of his ideas were the same as those already described in this chapter—encouraging the playing of instruments, honoring notations, and providing examples of notations. What was most significant to me about his thinking was that, with only a bit of input on my part, he quite eloquently and effortlessly came up with those things that I have identified. If an observant parent, not a musician himself, can see these things, then perhaps the gap between print and language, and music and sound, is a relatively simple one to bridge once the first foundation is set.

Private Music Lessons

It would seem that one of the most natural places to encourage children to compose and develop their own notational systems is in the context of the private music lesson—the after school, once a week trip to the local piano or guitar teacher that so many thousands of children routinely take. (This was abundantly clear to my neighbor as well.) Yet, it is unfortunately all too rare for children in private lessons to engage in composition as part of the regular lesson. The emphasis on perfecting performance is fed by the formal music conservatory traditions. I know all too well from my own experience how very easy it is to get caught up in learning the "proper" repertoire, preparing for exams, developing ensembles with other musicians, and preparing concerts. All of these things are exciting and important. But they should never be to the exclusion of time for exploration, improvisation, composition, and sheer play.

I have a dozen private piano pupils, and I was trained in a standard conservatory fashion. I am an active member of our provincial Registered Music Teachers Association, and now, as an adult, take lessons in both 'cello and in voice. In other words, I am firmly entrenched in the private music system. Recently, I was invited to speak at the annual meeting of a group of local music teachers belonging to the Registered Music Teachers Association. I was determined to use the opportunity to talk about the things I am writing about in this book, particularly as they relate to private music teaching. I was unsure as to what the response might be. Would the teachers see this as peripheral to the "real work" of educating performers? And an even greater concern—would they regard children's compositions and notations as trivial? I need not have worried. Without exception, the teachers were captivated by the children's work, and eager to see how their own students would respond if they were given both the means and the license to compose. Many realized that they were in a perfect position to encourage children's composition. After all, the private music lesson is truly an example of gourmet teaching, for it is a one-on-one, often long-term relationship, guided by the needs and wishes of both student and teacher. I was most gratified by the response of one of the most exacting matriarchs of the group, someone whom we all held in awe for her considerable talent as a teacher and unwavering performance expectations of her students. She, I thought, would likely be one of the most difficult to reach. But the look on her face, when examining notations of the kind that are scattered throughout this book, was one of enchantment. She, and others, have since pursued making composition a part of private music lessons, both through the kind of simple activity described earlier, and others that are described in later chapters (see Chapter 5 in particular). The beauty of introducing improvisation and composition as a part of the private music lesson is that not only is composition then made an integral part of learning to play the instrument, but the children also come to see how composition and performance are connected, thereby often enhancing their performances as well.

Specialist Music Programs
and the Regular Classroom

Music programs provided by school music specialists frequently share features of private music lessons but, unfortunately, are often watered-down *en masse* versions that are less than fulfilling for both children and teachers. Again, as in private music instruction, the emphasis tends to be on performance rather than on creation. Many elementary school music programs consist of singing by rote, and not much more (Borstad 1990; Gale 1990). In some cases there may be small instrument ensembles (e.g., recorder groups, and less often, string ensembles), but again the emphasis, indeed, the exclusive occupation of these groups is to learn repertoire to perform, rather than to create new music. As with the private music lessons geared to educating performers, there is nothing inherently wrong in this approach. In fact, belonging to an instrumental or choral group is often a highlight of school music, and even of school. The problem, as I see it, lies in the fact that the notion of creating one's own music is simply not addressed.

When I have asked both school music specialists and regular classroom teachers who have little experience in teaching music to explain why they shy away from teaching composition to their students, they typically give the same responses. It is interesting that the reasons put forth by both kinds of teachers are more alike than different—you cannot tell what someone teaches by the answers they give. And the reasons? For one, there is the age-old problem of viewing composition as something special, something that only a few people will ever attempt. I have discussed this earlier in the chapter and won't repeat myself here. The second reason that I commonly encounter is that the teachers themselves—both music specialists and classroom teachers—argue that they are not composers, so how can they teach composition? Part of the problem here is that people are imagining colossal symphonies as the only legitimate or "real" forms of composition, not realizing that the act of composition, and therefore exploration of notation, can occur on a much more modest scale. But perhaps the greatest impediment to teaching composition, and therefore to providing opportunities for notations to develop, is that it is difficult to imagine how this might be accomplished with a full class of students. How can 25 or 30 kids be creative at the same time, in different directions, using different instruments, and taking different developmental paths? I believe it can be done, and I will detail activities that work in large group situations throughout the last three chapters of this book. I have already outlined one such activity in this chapter. There are countless more ways to accommodate a classroom full of composers and notators, of any age and ability, once a teacher decides this is something worthwhile to do.

Using Different Instruments for Improvisation and Composition with a Class of Students

Closing Remarks
on Creating Environments

While I have described some of the materials, activities, and approaches that I have found to be fruitful in discovering children's notational abilities and nurturing the same, I have said little about the kinds of interventions teachers might make as they watch children at work, or better yet, work alongside their students. The nature of the kinds of interventions that might be made are discussed at length in later chapters (see Chapters 4 and 5). First, I would like to describe in some detail the kinds of notations that one might expect to find in any of the settings detailed in this chapter. Then, a discussion of interventions will undoubtedly be more meaningful, not only in terms of the kinds of interventions you may choose to use or adapt, but even more important, in terms of those that you may, as a result of reading the next few chapters, invent for yourself.

The Development of Children's Invented Music Notations

▲▲▲▲▲▲▲▲▲▲▲▲▲▲▲▲▲ I⊤ would take a lifetime to describe all of the possible paths that individual children might take in developing their knowledge of notational systems and their ability to use those systems. The path taken by any given child is affected by numerous elements in his or her environment—the musical diet in the home, the extent that the child is exposed to music of various cultures, the availability of instruments, the kinds of music teaching the child experiences, the child's general grasp of symbol systems, performance opportunities, and the way that the child views himself or herself as a learner, as a musician, and as a composer. While these factors sometimes create frustratingly great diversity in development, it is also possible to describe development in terms of the factors themselves, thereby bringing some order to the complexity of information in this area.

In this chapter and the next, I will consider a number of things that affect notational development. My choice is undoubtedly somewhat idiosyncratic, since it is driven by my own development in understanding children's notational systems. Thus, in the process of describing some of the research in this area, I will also describe the shift in my own research questions and teaching practices as I have come to understand more about the development of children's notational systems,[1] for what one understands is inherently linked to what one is able to see (based on the questions one asks) and nurture (based on the practices one adopts).

Although the factors I have chosen to structure this chapter by no means represent all of the forces at play in the development of notational knowledge, they encompass a growing body of examples, stories, practices, and research that together portray the scope and depth of development of children's notations. Thus, while my choices are personal ones, they are also supported by research in the field, through the work of others who are as interested as I in issues of notation.

The factors used to frame the research on children's notational systems will include: (1) the effects of music training, both with respect to the children's choices of symbols and to the kinds of information notated, (2) the effects of encouraging children to become composers and honoring their attempts at notating musical ideas, and (3) the instruments that children use for improvisation and composition. The third of these forms the basis of the next chapter. In addition, general cognitive growth, particularly in terms of symbol systems and learning environments, is considered in Appendix A.

Music Training

One of the first features of children's music environments that concerned researchers and teachers alike was the effect of music training on children's music perceptions, performances, and notations. In terms of notation, much of the early work was undertaken in the area of rhythm. What do children do when asked to notate a rhythm sequence? Is their response different if they have had music training, particularly training in reading standard notation?

---

[1]These shifts in research questions and teaching practices are rarely discussed in formal journal articles, some of which I refer to at length in the present chapter. But these shifts, nevertheless, are often the most revealing, and deserve acknowledgment and description.

In the early 1980s, Jeanne Bamberger designed an ingenious task. She asked children to listen to a clapped rhythm sequence, and then to "put down on paper whatever you think will help you remember the . . . piece tomorrow or help someone else to play it who isn't here today" (Bamberger 1982, 194). From this simple task, an enormous amount of research was generated. In the past decade, our understanding of children's knowledge of rhythm has evolved considerably, by building on Bamberger's elegant work.

When Bamberger asked children to notate some simple rhythm sequences, she found an intriguing phenomenon. Children with music training tended to respond to the **metric** aspects of rhythm, while children without music training, and indeed, untrained adults as well, were more likely to respond to the figural aspects of rhythm. That is, people who had training in music would usually respond to the underlying regular metered structure of a clapped sequence, representing each clap in terms of a measured underlying beat. Thus, a clap that was twice as long as another would be notated in some way to indicate this relationship, regardless of where the claps occurred in the rhythm sequence. For instance, a clap worth "two" might be drawn twice as large as a clap worth "one."

In contrast, children without music training represented each clap in terms of the claps around it, showing the figures or chunks rather than the absolute measured relationships between claps. Thus, a clap of "two" might be drawn with the same symbol as a clap worth "one" if the "two" clap occurred after a series of claps worth "one." In the classic example in Figure 3–1, a child with music training would represent the claps in terms of their absolute durations (shorts and longs), regardless of where the claps occurred in the sequence. A child without music training, however, would represent the groups (or figures) of claps formed by the proximity of long and short durations in relation to each other. In this way, a child without music training would likely represent a long clap as short, if the long clap came after two short claps, which made the long clap *sound* short.

The most profound implication of Bamberger's research is that while music teachers typically teach standard music notation, which embodies the metric aspects of rhythm, children without training—most of the children in a classroom—naturally respond to the figural aspects of rhythm. Therefore, not only are we asking them to think in unfamiliar terms, which is bad enough, but we

Standard music notation

In this notation, the metric nature of the rhythm is captured by the use of eighth and quarter notes, and the figures are marked by slurs. Pitch is also shown by the relative placement of the notes on the staff.

Standard rhythm notation

This notation differs from the one above in that only the rhythm (both metric and figural, as indicated by the slurs) is shown.

Two examples of figural rhythm notations

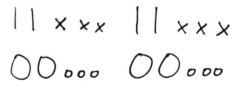

Two examples of metric rhythm notations

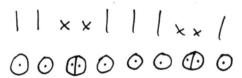

even fail to honor the rhythm knowledge that they have—figural knowledge that could be used to help them achieve metric or formal understanding.

I was both deeply affected by Bamberger's work and curious as to where it might lead. By the time I encountered her research in 1982, I had been teaching piano for about ten years. I was shocked to think that I had spent so many years teaching piano, and in so doing, teaching about rhythm and durations, without having any idea of what the children I was teaching *understood* of rhythm. If I had thought about it, I would have realized that children already had a wealth of rhythm understanding when they came for lessons. They could keep time to a piece of music (a metric skill), and they could often clap back a rhythm sequence or sing a song that had many different durations with accuracy (both figural and metric skills). But rather than relating their understanding to the new material I was teaching them, linking their performance skills to a new symbol system, I would, as many others do, simply launch into an explanation of quarter notes and eighth notes in 4/4 time.

When I was introduced to the work of Bamberger, it was a happy coincidence that at the time I was a graduate student in search of a dissertation topic. The research I came to develop for the dissertation focused on children's understanding of rhythm. I worked with both musically trained and untrained children, from the ages of seven to twelve years, and presented them with many tasks, expanding on Bamberger's earlier work. Besides asking children to represent rhythms as described above, I had them clap from other rhythm notations, keep time to music, represent beats, and listen for congruities between melodies and beats. In other words, I tried to design a variety of related tasks so that I could assess not only the effects of music training, but also begin to look at how skill at one kind of task (say, a motor task) was related to skill on other tasks (say, symbolic or aural) (Upitis 1985, 1987a).

The findings from my first study on rhythm notation were extensive. But much more important, the findings strongly influenced, and continue to influence, how I teach aspects of rhythm (see Chapters 4 and 5). What I found has also influenced how I go about notating rhythm when I am composing—I am now far more comfortable using figural notation, later translating it to metric terms. Similarly, I often use figural groupings when learning a difficult rhythm for a vocal or piano composition, rather than trying to make sense of the rhythm metrically. Other researchers have

All of the invented notations below depict the following rhythm:

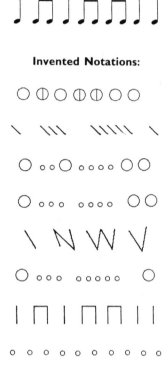

Invented Notations:

pursued this line of inquiry, focusing on related issues such as the features of the rhythm sequences themselves and the extent of individual differences within a broad developmental pattern (e.g., Smith 1989).

But back to the research findings. I mentioned previously that the tasks I designed touched several kinds of understanding—motor, aural, and symbolic. Not surprisingly, since I had the children engage in a huge variety of rhythm activities—there were 42 measures for each child—I found that *no* children could be classified as having either purely metric understanding or purely figural understanding. Rather, all children understood aspects of both figural and metric features of rhythm. While children with music training favored metric descriptions, they would also respond figurally in some instances. For example, when asking children to read a "mystery rhythm" (see Figure 3–2), many children with music training used figural descriptions to make sense of a new rhythm. Children were given the page of drawings depicted in Figure 3–2, and told that they were to "guess the mystery rhythm by clapping it, picking out the one that you find easiest to read" (Upitis 1985, 81). When subsequently asked which drawing(s) "helped you figure out the rhythm" (Upitis 1985, 81), many children with music training used figural representations to clap the mystery rhythm. In fact, all of the representations, with the exception of the last, were used by at least some of the children in decoding the rhythm pattern, indicating that a great variety of notations could be used to make sense of the same rhythm.

I don't want to leave you with the impression that children's representations of rhythm patterns are always simply classified as figural or metric. Within each category, there is a great deal of variation. Also, some drawings, though not many, are ambiguous—it is simply not clear what the child has intended in the description (Smith 1989). Consequently, researchers in this field have spent a good deal of time attempting to create a typology that could be used to classify children's representations of rhythm (e.g., Bamberger 1982; Davidson & Scripp 1988a; Hildebrandt 1985; Upitis 1987a). I worked first from Bamberger's typology, modifying it after analyzing the results from my research. Davidson and Scripp (1988a) have suggested further modifications (see Figure 3–3). While we have not reached unanimous agreement as to the natural development of children's spontaneous notations of rhythm, and perhaps we never will, several things are no longer in dispute. First, children's spontaneous or invented notations of rhythm begin with what have been termed rhythmic scribbles or icons or pictures representing the act of clapping. One of my favorites is pictured in Figure 3–4. What better way to show the memory of a rhythm? Later, children make marks to show discrete events (e.g., they make a drawing showing that seven claps were heard, but fail to differentiate between short and long claps). From this, children may then move to figural or metric descriptions, and these descriptions themselves become more sophisticated. Perhaps the most important thing to bear in mind as one is looking at children's descriptions is that their developmental paths are never simple, and never either solely figural or metric. I once made the argument

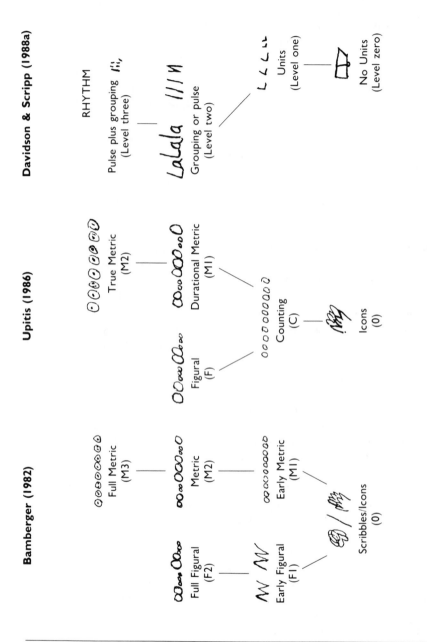

FIGURE 3–3 *Three typologies for invented rhythm notations*
(The Upitis and Bamberger typologies appear in an earlier article, Upitis 1987a.)

FIGURE 3-4 *An invented rhythm notation using a picture*
(From Upitis 1985.)

The child, when asked to "draw something so that you remember the rhythm," has drawn a picture of himself clapping the sequence, and the "memory" of clapping the sequence.

that the two types of understanding develop in tandem (Upitis 1987a). While the specifics of this claim have been questioned (e.g., Smith 1989), many still believe that at any stage of development, a child will be able to demonstrate both figural and metric knowledge, if a variety of tasks are considered.

Having spent some years looking at children's understanding of rhythm, and being both fascinated and a bit frightened by the complexity of the field (my doctoral dissertation was over 300 pages long, and yikes! I had only looked at rhythm understanding in children from the ages of seven to twelve), it was with some hesitation that I began to look at children's understanding of melody. Others were already working in this field. For some time, Lyle Davidson and his colleagues at Harvard's Project Zero had been examining children's representations of melody. Not surprisingly, there are a number of parallels between children's invented notations of melody and those of rhythm.

In 1988, Davidson and Scripp reported the results of a three-year longitudinal study on the representation of a melodic fragment—the last phrase of *Row, Row, Row Your Boat* (see Figure 3-5). While they were only examining the representations made

FIGURE 3–5 *The melodic fragment of* Row, Row, Row Your Boat *used by Davidson and Scripp (1988a)*

Life   is but   a dream.

by young children without formal music training, it is significant that they found parallel developments in pitch and rhythm. Children appear to pay attention to features of the melody like contour and **intervals** before encoding discrete pitches in more absolute or, in Davidson's and Scripp's terminology, regulated terms. This is somewhat like responding to figures in rhythmic sequences before dealing with relative durations in metric terms. Again, what we draw attention to in teaching (e.g., "This is F in the treble clef") may not correspond with children's intuitive sense of melody.

A later study by Davidson, Scripp, and Welsh (1988) reveals a disturbing but remarkable result with respect to the effects of music training on the notation of melody. When Davidson, Scripp, and Welsh asked conservatory students—people who had spent many years studying their instrument—to write out the melody of *Happy Birthday* using standard notation, very few were able to do this correctly (see Figure 3–6). One would think that after reading notation successfully for an extended period of time, writing a simple melody would be a simple matter. But it is not. I have observed this in my own practice. I will never forget my surprise when I first saw a child, who had been reading standard notation for five years, put stems on the wrong sides of the notes when writing her own composition. How, I wondered, could someone who had been using the standard system for so long make that kind of error? But as Davidson and Scripp (1988b) argue, this lack of integrated literacy skills after many years of instrumental lessons occurs because literacy skills are only acquired as needed. If students have not had reason to integrate reading with other aspects of literacy (writing, discriminating between the score and the performance, and so on), then they are likely to, as Davidson and Scripp (1988b) put it, "compensate for the lack of integration in

Happy Birthday in correct standard notation:

Notations by entering conservatory students:

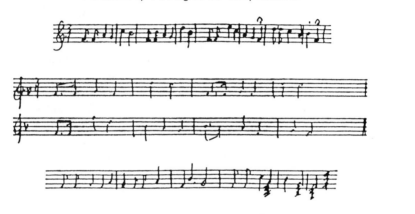

their training by substituting 'what they know about music' for what they hear" (p. 77). Thus, in the *Happy Birthday* example, students often begin and end the song on the same note because most simple melodies follow that form, even though in this case, *Happy Birthday* begins on a note other than the **tonic** (home key). Davidson and Scripp (1988b) further argue that integration between music literacy and performance skills is more likely to occur when the environment links performance, representation, and composition, and where there is an emphasis on solving musical problems.

Observations like these made me think that while the research described thus far had been fruitful in terms of understanding how training in standard notation affects how children represent rhythm and melody, it still gave a very limited view of the development of notational systems. As time went on, I realized that there were at least two things about the research of the kind I have described that I found limiting, and indeed, disturbing. For one, I had spent a good deal of time teaching music in public schools in inner-city environments, both in Canada and in the United States.[2] In those schools, most of the children would never have the opportunity to take private lessons outside of school, so it seemed that spending a good deal of effort understanding the effects of music training on children's notational systems was out of place when almost none of the children I was dealing with would ever have the opportunity to have such instruction. In other words, I felt that the research emphasizing music training was in some sense elitist— an attitude towards music that I had been trying to fight for many years. Yet, in a significant way, I was perpetuating this through my own research. Besides, what did the years of training at a conservatory level do for people's ability to write as opposed to read notation? As a result of concerns such as these, I became more interested in looking at the similarities rather than the differences in development, and further, looking at the growing knowledge of a particular child rather than comparing one group to another.

The second limiting factor from my perspective came from the realization that much of the research, indeed, *most* of the research on the effects of music training on perception, production, notation, and performance, looked at how children were able to represent *other* people's rhythms and melodies, but not their own. I was more interested in something else, namely, how notational systems would develop in an environment where children were composers, and thus would develop notations as they needed them to record and edit their own works. How would children develop notational systems when it was in the context of their own work? Would they be better at using standard notation if they were using it for composition? And more generally, how could this development be described in terms of the symbols in other fields, such as language and mathematics? I could not help but be impressed and influenced by the massive movements of change we witnessed since the late 1970s in the fields of language, mathematics, and science (see, for example, Atwell 1987; Goodman 1986; Graves 1983;

---

[2]See *This Too Is Music* (Upitis 1990) where my role as a music teacher in one of these schools in Boston, Massachusetts, is discussed at length.

Mills & Clyde 1990; Newman 1983, in language; Baker & Baker 1990; Whitin, Mills, & O'Keefe 1990, in mathematics; and Osborne & Freyberg 1985, in science). It has now become acceptable, and even expected, that children will be given the opportunity to approach mathematics through manipulating real world materials and solving real world problems. Similarly, children are learning to write by becoming writers. How could the very positive aspects of these movements, particularly the whole language movement, be related to music teaching and learning? How important is the audience to children—do they think about who will read their story or play their music? I turn now to a discussion based on questions such as these.

Inventing Notational Systems: The Role of Composition

Without getting too buried in technical detail and academic prose (I hope!), I will devote the rest of this chapter to a look at development of notational systems. In so doing, I will also pay attention to the context in which the notations are generated. How do children view themselves as composers? How much of what children notate reflects what they know? How do they view other children and adults in an environment where compositions are shared? How does development in other symbols systems, such as spelling, relate to music notations? Throughout the discussion, there will be lots of examples of notations, and, in amongst all of the research, stories about a particular child named Joel.

Children's Views of Themselves as Composers and the Role of Others

Children view themselves as writers long before they view themselves as readers. That is, children see themselves as able to generate notations of music and text of language before they can make sense of similar representations made by others. Bissix (1980) describes her son as a writer before he was a reader. Similarly, Joel, at the age of five years, thought of himself as a composer of music but not as a reader of music. He would happily improvise music on different instruments and notate some of his improvisations, but he did not believe that he would ever be able to "read those notes that Mommy does." This is in keeping with Graves's (1983) report that most six-year-olds (90 percent) believe that they can write, while only 15 percent believe that they can read.

Given that children view themselves as writers and composers, the use that they make of symbols in those roles becomes of crucial interest—more interesting, I think, than their understanding of other people's symbols, including standard music notation.[3] Predictably, this is strongly affected by the instruments that the children play. That is, the instruments used for improvisation, composition, and performance, are from the beginning linked to the generation of symbols, and remain so. Just as Hawkins (1974) acknowledges that children could take many different paths in exploring a new idea in science, children may take different paths in developing symbol systems. Borrowing from other systems, they may develop iconic systems, numeric systems, alphabetic systems, alpha-numeric systems, or graphic systems. Examples of all of these kinds of symbols, and combinations of them, appear throughout this book. But, as Hawkins argues further, when the time comes to move away from the "messing about" into more directed inquiries, it should be possible for children to pursue the path they have identified during the messing about stage. Thus, a child who has begun with a numeric system should be able to pursue that system in later explorations, and indeed, should be given help in that pursuit. The many ways that teachers can encourage these kinds of explorations are given in Chapter 5.

When considering children's music notations, one should also bear in mind that children do not necessarily notate everything that they know about a given melody or rhythm. Polanyi (1958) claimed that we know more than we can articulate. Similarly, examining children's notations does not necessarily give a full picture of their ability to represent music. In fact, the opposite is probably true. Thus, it is important, as with the "mystery rhythm" task described previously, to give children many opportunities to use and make sense of various systems, both for decoding and encoding music—the more they articulate, the more they find that they know. Children have a remarkable ability to move in and out of various systems, and by doing so, they learn more about all of the systems they encounter and invent.

---

[3]See the discussion in Appendix A regarding toys, tools, and symbols, and cycles of learning, where it is argued that there is an ongoing oscillation between exploration and precision, between using tools and generating symbols.

Children may move in and out of different systems for some time before refining their use of symbols. The need for refining a notational system, and in so doing, standardizing the use of symbols, comes when there is a desire to communicate to people who will have only the notation to work from. I stated earlier (see Chapter 2) that the creation of music notations came at a time when musicians began to travel, and therefore shared notated music with others. I also observed that personal history mirrors this development. Thus, children four or five years of age often strongly resist standardizing their symbols because they have no perceived need to do so. Simply put, while these children may realize that they use one symbol in different ways, they see no problem in doing this, since they can't imagine not having the chance to explain to the reader which interpretation should be used. A story about Joel illustrates this point (from Upitis 1987b).

When Joel was five years old, he asked for piano lessons. At the time, I was keenly interested in children's notations of their own melodies. Since I knew his mother well, I convinced her that it might be more interesting to approach the piano through a combination of improvisation, composition, and, if the timing was right, more formal note reading. In this context, Joel was able to develop his abilities as a beginning composer, meeting with me quite regularly over a couple of years, to "do some things at the piano."

Joel was surrounded by a house full of music, and as such, had a good understanding of what music symbols looked like. Predictably, however, he used standard music symbols in nonstandard ways. One instance of this was Joel's practice of using the eighth note pair for two different purposes. Sometimes he would use the eighth note pair both to signify two notes playing at once. Other times, he would use it to represent two notes played in sequence. At one point, I confronted him with this ambiguity, asking "How can you tell they're different from your music?" He answered, "Well, it isn't different, but I just showed you." When I asked him what would happen if he wasn't there, Joel grew frustrated and puzzled, since clearly he *was* there. The following interchange occurred:

> JOEL: You mean what happened if you weren't here and you wanted that thingie [meaning the two notes together]? And I was with them [i.e., the hypothetical person]?
> RENA: No, you weren't with the person either. All the person had was your music.

JOEL: You mean me and you and me were away and I was outside playing baseball?

RENA: Yes.

JOEL: You mean how would they know not to do this [plays two C♯s in a row]?

RENA: Yes.

JOEL: You see, someone is obviously in the house.

RENA: What if there was no one in the house?

JOEL: Well, I always come in for a drink, and I'd notice them. I'd come out of the kitchen with my cup full of juice and um, come in here with my glass, I mean my cup full of juice, and all I'll do it sort of like, and you know, watch and stuff and sit around and *turn around and show them.*

Some time later, when using the eighth note pair again, Joel must have remembered the conversation described above, for he both demonstrated and instructed, "You can play two notes here [meaning simultaneously] *or* two notes each time [meaning sequentially]. You can do it any way you want to." So much for the ambiguity.

To sum, it is important when reading about notational development in the part that follows, to bear in mind that all of the notations generated, whether in a composition context or in response to a research task, were generated by children who likely had strong views about themselves as composers, children who could work with more than one symbol system, and children who probably had thoughts about the audience for both their pieces and their notations. These notations were created by real children— complicated creatures that they are.

Stages of Notational Development— The Sources

Although "stages" sounds like I am about to weave a tight predictable pattern of notational development, in reality the weave is a loose one. I have patched together many odd bits of fabric— examples from the work of Davidson and his colleagues where children were asked to notate a given melody, examples from researchers such as Gentry who are interested in children's invented spellings, and of course, examples from my own teaching and research. Most of the latter examples were created by children as they were producing notations that would capture the pieces they had composed. Some of these compositions were created on keyboards, some on percussion instruments such as tambourines and drums, and some on Orff xylophones. So while the weave might be a loose one, the fabrics are all colorful ones, and in this arrangement at least, all have a place.

Many of the children's notations for their own compositions were produced using a common approach. Although this approach has already been described in the previous chapter, I will add a few words here to remind you of the approach.

When I begin working with children, I first give them as long as they need—and want—to "play around" on the instruments. In some cases, this takes the children many hours. Others are ready to start writing after a few minutes. Sometimes I give children specific ideas for guiding their improvisations, especially for the more complex keyboard instruments such as piano and synthesizer (see Chapter 5). In other instances, no initial guidance is given. In all cases, however, once the children have settled into their instrument, they are asked to "make up a piece, and then write it down so that you can remember it or so that someone else could read it." They are then encouraged to trade their notations around, having others read from their work, as they try reading the notations of their friends. From this activity a wealth of notations are generated, many of which are now described.

Stages of Notation and Spelling: Davidson and Gentry

The typology proposed by Davidson and Scripp (1988a), based on the notations made by children of other people's melodies, suggests that children move from no units or pictures (Level 0), to units of some kind (Level 1), to the description of melodic contour and/or intervallic boundaries in the case of pitch, and pulse or grouping in the case of rhythm (Level 2), and finally, to the description of regulated pitches and integrated pulse and grouping (Level 3). The latter three of these stages roughly parallel the semiphonetic, phonetic, and transitional stages of invented spellings identified by Gentry (1982). When children's notations of their *own* compositions are included, generated in the manner just described, music notations that parallel the first spelling stage (precommunicative) and last stage (correct) are evidenced as well. These two typologies are now described in detail. (Don't worry, it will all make more sense tomorrow—especially if you go out there and have a child notate a piece or two!)

Precommunicative—Early Communicative/Iconic

Examples of precommunicative spelling and what can be seen as a parallel stage in music notation for children who have been exposed to music symbols have already been illustrated in the previous chapter (see Figure 2–1). Further examples appear in Figure 3–7. It was argued earlier that just as the child in the precommunicative stage makes strings of letters that don't form words, the child who plays with music symbols creates combinations that don't make melodies. Gentry (1982) has shown that at this very earliest level of spelling development, children demonstrate that they have some knowledge of the alphabet, even though they appear to have no knowledge of letter-sound correspondence.

The use of music symbols shown in Figure 3–7 can be described in similar terms. Obviously the child has some knowledge of standard music symbols, and understands that they have meaning, but the child does not understand how a given symbol represents pitch or duration. The child may well use one music symbol to represent an entire piece of music. In some cases the child is merely playing with symbols—"drawing music for fun," as one child put it. At this stage, the child may or may not understand that music, like text, is also read from left to right. Further, the child may make drawings, letters, and numbers to accompany the

---

FIGURE 3–7 *Precommunicative spelling and an early music notation*

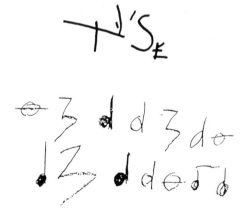

---

symbols of music. In the same way that a precommunicative speller mixes upper and lowercase letters, the child playing with the symbols of music mixes symbols of various types of meaning (e.g., different durations, clefs).

Because Davidson and his colleagues did not include settings where children were learning about music symbols, their first stage of invented notation differs substantially from the other invented music notation pictured in Figure 3–7. The stage they identify as the "no units" stage (Level 0) essentially represents children's attempts at writing *something* down—an icon or a picture—presumably in part because this is the expectation of the researcher. Other researchers, including myself, have called this stage the "iconic" stage (Upitis 1990a; Linton 1991). But I would argue that the music notation in Figure 3–7 is qualitatively different from the iconic stage depicted in Figure 3–8. Like the precommunicative speller, the child making the notation with music symbols in Figure 3–7 is aware of an "alphabet"—some of the symbols of standard music notation, unlike the child making a "no units" or iconic notation where no knowledge of music symbols is demonstrated.

Semiphonetic—Units

At the semiphonetic stage of spelling development, Gentry (1982) found that children first begin to understand the notation of an alphabet, where letters are related to sounds. Here the representation of the words may be phonetic, but in an abbreviated form (see Figure 3–9). For instance, semiphonetic spellers may use one letter for an entire word, particularly if the word sounds like the letter (e.g., *R* for *are*). These children understand that text is read from left to right, but may or may not segment words.

FIGURE 3–8 *"Iconic" or "no units" notations*

No units (Davidson & Scripp 1988a)   Iconic (Upitis 1985)

FIGURE 3-9 *Semiphonetic spelling*

Semiphonetic spelling (Bissex 1980)

RUDF   BRDE

[Are you deaf?]   [birdie]

At the level of units (Level 1) identified by Davidson and Scripp (1988a), the child begins to represent discrete notes with separate symbols (see Figure 3–10). Like a child at the semiphonetic stage of spelling, however, these representations may sometimes be made for each note, but as often as not, the child may use only one symbol for an entire phrase, similar to a child using one letter to represent an entire word. Children who are using standard notation symbols, but only capturing unit information, make similar notations at this stage. The eighth note pair used by Joel would fall under this category, where his use of standard notation symbols was limited to a counting or unit function.

Children at this stage of notation development usually make notations that are to be read from left to right. In music, however, when more than one note is being played at the same time, there is also a vertical dimension. When children are creating their own

FIGURE 3-10 *Invented notations at the "units" level*

Units (Davidson & Scripp 1988a)

Notation   Melody

Life is but a dream.

Units using music symbols (Upitis 1985)

Notation   Rhythm Pattern

---

compositions, and not responding to a given melodic fragment, they often have difficulty representing the vertical dimension at this stage (e.g., showing which notes are to be played at the same time by different instruments; see Figure 3–11). Even if they manage to portray two instruments playing at the same time as in Figure 3–12—which I think is often purely by chance—they may have difficulty following their notation when a friend plays the second instrument.

Another interesting way of confusing the standard vertical dimension was demonstrated by Joel. (Joel's "confusions" were always interesting—and made a good deal of sense once I could figure out his system.)

Many of Joel's first compositions were based on the black note pentatonic scale, taking inspiration from the question and answer improvisatory game we played on the black keys (see Chapter 5). For several weeks Joel carefully notated the number of notes in his piece, paying little if any attention to relative durations or pitch. His notations, therefore, were clearly at the units stage—"how many" notes was more important than "which notes." Because of Joel's familiarity with standard notation symbols, he almost always used conventional looking notation to make his unit representations. While he would indicate pitch if I asked him to, the important issues for Joel remained "how many" and the use of "real notes."

FIGURE 3–11   *An inaccurate attempt at representing two instruments playing at once*

FIGURE 3-12 *An accurate notation for two instruments playing at once*

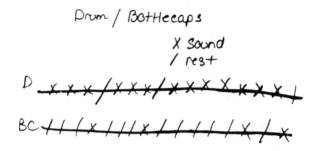

For instance, in the notation pictured in Figure 3–13, Joel drew a picture of the black keys in response to my asking where the tune was to be played. Later, when I referred to the picture of the black keys as "notes," he emphatically stated, "Those *aren't* the notes. See, there's no ball. Those are just where you play," fortifying my observation that Joel was using conventional symbols only for counting, and not for pitch or duration.

The composition in Figure 3–14 illustrates yet another way that Joel used standard notation as a counting or units device. While I was aware that Joel was writing the notes vertically because he had seen **chords** notated elsewhere, I also knew that he meant for each note to be played separately. He was thrilled with the power of the notation, and with making a "long song." His original composition had six notes, but when he went to write it down, he accidentally drew seven circles. After counting them, he commented, "Oops. Seven. I meant to say seven . . . This time maybe ten. Maybe twenty!" After writing the "long song with twenty notes," I played from Joel's notation by reading it in the conventional way, that is, playing all twenty notes at once, by leaning with both elbows on the keyboard. This brought on a strongly negative reaction from Joel, "No, no, no, no, no. You're not supposed to put your arm on there. You have to *count* them." Joel then added a large circle to the bottom of the twenty notes, a zero to help me count. He explained that the zero was not to be played, but was to be regarded as a "starting point." In other words, Joel was using every symbol system he knew to make a unit notation—

FIGURE 3–13 *Using a picture of the black keys to represent pitches*

The invented notation (black keys were added after the child
was asked which notes to play):

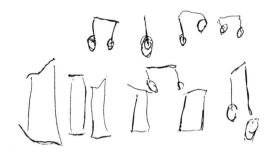

The piece as it would appear in standard notation:

"and then you keep going up"

standard music symbols (in a non-standard way), as well as a
mathematical symbol (in a correspondingly non-standard way).

Phonetic—Contour/Intervals/Grouping or Pulse

At the phonetic stage, children systematically represent the sounds
of the words through their spelling (see Figure 3–15). Finally!—
words that many of us can read, if not fluently, at least with a little
work. Letters are assigned on the basis of the sound they make,
without regard for conventions of letter sequence or orthography
(Gentry 1982). At this stage, children also develop consistent ways
of dealing with recurring details (e.g., *-ed* endings) and are aware
of word segmentation.

The corresponding stage of invented music notation development is extremely difficult to describe, and the notations are
harder to read than phonetic spellings. In fact, there are times when
I wonder why I spend time trying to classify the notations of this
complicated, intriguing, in-between stage. A part of me screams

FIGURE 3–14 *Using standard notation for counting or "units"*
(This figure appears in Upitis 1987b, p. 109.)

The child's invented notation (indicates the number of notes,
but not the pitches or durations):

The piece as it would appear in standard notation:

in frustration when I have 55 notations in front of me that belong
in what I can see as 47 distinct categories. A bigger part of me is
secretly pleased that these notations and the children who made
them seem to defy classification, and so, I merrily go on trying to
understand the notation of the moment, or the developmental
pattern within a single child.

It is no wonder that these notations are difficult to classify,
and to compare with invented spellings. At this stage, the inherent
differences between music and words become most apparent, as
children now grapple with the complexities of notating pitch and
rhythm, and when composing their own pieces, deal with texture,

FIGURE 3–15 *Phonetic spelling*

"Gee, Hallowe'en is
here," said Molly.
We've got to
get ready
for it. Molly
was so excited
that she
could hardly
wait
until
it was time.

"Ge HALAWeN'L
HeR" 2AD MALe.
weV GOT to
GAT RADe
f OR iT! MALe
WAZLO iKSiTiD
TAtZE
KODHARLe
WAto
UNtiL
it WAZTiM.

mood, repetitions, and **dynamics** as well. So, rather than forcing parallels where perhaps none exist, I will instead give examples to try and capture the diversity and ingenuity of children's work at this stage. And of course, I'll tell a story about Joel, to more deeply characterize this stage.

At this middle, muddled stage of music notation, one child may notate rhythmic groupings consistently, but be unable to describe those groupings in terms of pulse. Conversely, another child may notate the pulse without showing the figural groups. In the case of melody, there is some indication that the child understands the shape of the melody at this stage, and even the relationship of one note to the next in terms of pitch. He or she may nevertheless still be unable to consistently notate both rhythm and pitch in such a way as to allow a reader to reproduce the melody from the notation (see Figure 3–16). Again, as with spelling, much of the music "grammar" is in place—children realize that in notating rhythm, pulse and groupings are important, and that in notating pitch, intervals and contour are salient. Similarly in spelling, children have developed rules for dealing with certain kinds of word endings, but not necessarily in conventional ways.

FIGURE 3-16 *Notating aspects of pitch and/or rhythm in systematic ways*

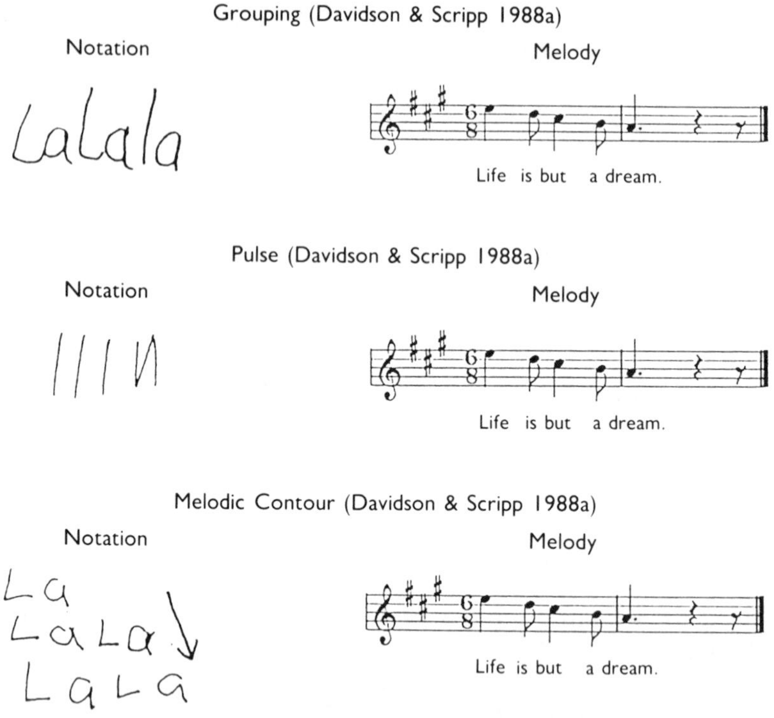

Grouping (Davidson & Scripp 1988a)

Notation | Melody

Life is but a dream.

Pulse (Davidson & Scripp 1988a)

Notation | Melody

Life is but a dream.

Melodic Contour (Davidson & Scripp 1988a)

Notation | Melody

Life is but a dream.

If children are given more than one opportunity to notate a melody, however, that demonstrated consistency sometimes falls by the wayside. At this stage more than any other (whatever we decide to call this stage), I have found that children are most likely to notate the same music event through a series of different representations. This is also the stage where the ambiguous rhythm drawings referred to earlier (e.g., Smith 1989) are most likely to surface. It seems that multiple representations are frequently made when the child has trouble with a system, and tries several different ways to communicate the music message. For instance, when a seven-year-old was trying to notate *Twinkle, Twinkle, Little Star*, a very familiar melody, he tried first to use the letter *A* for quarter notes or full phrases, and the letter *B* for eighth notes. This proved too cumbersome, so he resorted to using words ("twikle little tikel star") and pictures of stars. He then tried using abstract graphic symbols for pitch placement, short lines indicating the relative pitches of the notes. This method was not entirely successful either, so he then began drawing wavy lines to show the texture and phrasing. Finally, after a good fifteen minutes of experimenting with different symbols and methods, he drew a page full of stars. Here, then, is a child who is well aware of the musical dimensions of the piece, but unable to combine all of them in one notation.

My friend Joel also moved away from using standard notation symbols when he became interested in other features of music besides the number of notes in his compositions. A few months after I started working with Joel, he became intrigued with ways that different moods could be portrayed on the piano, using its highest and lowest registers. He developed two consistent symbols for showing mood: a thick, dense figure for low music, and a looping figure for notes in the upper registers (see Figure 3–17). A further modification of this notation can be seen in Figure 3–18, where Joel not only uses his looping symbol for part of his melody, but also adds the word "LOW," and draws a picture of someone playing the piano, including a picture of a piano hammer striking the strings. This is a bit like the child described earlier who, in an attempt to notate everything about *Twinkle, Twinkle, Little Star*, used many notational devices to that end. Another interesting development that accompanied this new form of notation was that Joel had returned to creating his pieces at the piano, notating them later, as opposed to making the notation first and then playing from it to hear the result (as in the twenty-note piece in Figure 3–14).

Transitional—Regulated

When children reach the transitional stage of spelling, many conventions of English orthography are consistently represented (Gentry 1982). Vowels are used in every syllable, and children begin using such conventions as the silent *e* to make a long vowel sound (e.g., TIP [for type] becomes TIPE). Sometimes all letters are included, but not necessarily in the right order (e.g., HUOSE [for house]). Some simple words are consistently spelled correctly (e.g., HAT).

A child who has reached what Davidson and Scripp (1988a) identify as the stage of recording regulated pitches along with both pulse and grouping in a rhythm notation may be seen as operating

FIGURE 3–17 *Invented notations for a "low rumbling" and a "high looping" piece*
(Another version of this figure appears in Upitis 1987b, p. 109.)

Invented notation for the "low rumbling" piece:

The piece as it would appear in standard notation:

Invented notation for the "high looping" piece:

The piece as it would appear in standard notation:

FIGURE 3–18 *Using the "high looping" notation for a low piece, along with other symbols*
(Another version of this figure appears in Upitis 1987b, p. 111.)

The invented notation:

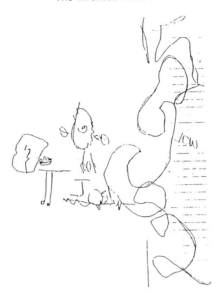

The piece as it would appear in standard notation:

at a transitional stage of invented music notations (see Figure 3–19). In some ways, these notations are already correct, in that they capture the essence of pitch and rhythm. Thus, just like the child who spells some words correctly and consistently, a child at this stage may notate some elements of a melody correctly and consistently, such as pulse and grouping. However, at this transitional stage, pitch, while regulated, is not absolute. In other words, while one can tell both the contour of the melody, and the relative pitch levels, one cannot re-construct *actual* pitches. Thus, one cannot tell, for instance, whether to start singing on a D or a G, although once the right starting position is found, the other pitches fall into place.

FIGURE 3–19 *Examples of regulated, though non-standard, invented music notations*

Regulated pitches (Davidson & Scripp 1988a)

Notation

Melody

Life is but a dream.

Figural Grouping using metric symbols (Upitis 1985)

Notation

Rhythm Pattern

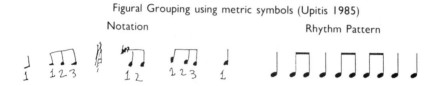

The invented notation:
(This figure appears in *This Too Is Music*: Upitis 1990b, p. 64.)

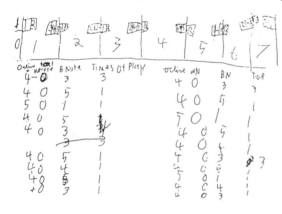

This child has notated not only what is to be played, but also what is not played (i.e., the white keys), giving a picture of the whole instrument.

The piece as it would appear in standard notation:

When children are creating notations in the context of composition, they develop transitional or regulated notations using symbols related to the instrument that they play. This notion is developed in the next chapter. For now, I will give yet another example from Joel's development to indicate how notations that are essentially transitional or regulated differ from those collected by Davidson and Scripp (1988a), where a given melody is notated. That is, when the notations are "contaminated" by real life—an instrument, school, interactions with siblings, and instruction from a teacher—different forms of transitional or regulated notations emerge.

Joel became interested in conventional notation again at around the same time that he came home after the second day of kindergarten in September, frustrated because he had not been taught how to read ("I go to school every day and I still don't know how to read"). This frustration extended to his music reading and writing as well. He asked his mother to teach him to read text, and he asked me to teach him to read music. Neither were easy tasks. One day, after battling with two notes in the treble clef (C and F), Joel commented in disgust, "I'm not like you. I don't have that many brains in my head. And also I'm not like my Mom either." But when I asked him if he'd like to make up a song, he responded, "Sure! If I have a pen and paper!" I suggested that he try something on the piano first, but he refused, saying "No. I want to do it in my brain on the paper. With Cs and Fs. And another C." Shortly after, Joel produced his version of *Silent Night* (see Figure 3–20). He insisted on printing the title (his mother wrote the title in dotted lines for him to trace), as well as asking his mother to draw in a treble clef to make it "real music." In fact, his very choice of melody—someone else's familiar melody—underscored his preoccupation with "real music." He ended the piece with a **double barline**, so "people will know it's the end."

For a very brief period, Joel produced a good number of notations like these—hardly what one would call transitional in Gentry's terms, or regulated in Davidson's and Scripp's typology. This, of course, is to be expected. Just because a child demonstrates a higher level of notation doesn't mean that he or she won't revert back to other notations when circumstances—like school—shape such a change. In this vein, Joel also returned to using quarter and eighth notes as counters, without any indication of pitch or relative duration. Perhaps he did this because that notation had once worked for him, and he was certainly frustrated with this reading

FIGURE 3–20 *An attempt at notating* Silent Night *using standard symbols*
(This figure appears in Upitis 1987b, p.113.)

and writing business, both at the piano and at school, so going back to an old notation probably made sense to him. From using this notation a second time, however, a significant change occurred. His older sister, upon encountering one of the units notations, confronted him, as only sisters can do. When she asked him what the notes were, and he told her G, she indignantly retorted with, "Well, how am I supposed to know that's a G?" Joel then grabbed a pencil and furiously added letters with each symbol (see Figure 3–21). Soon after, he must have realized that he could dispense with the quarter and eighth note symbols altogether, and use only letter names. For several months, Joel's compositions were notated in the form shown in Figure 3–22. His notations invariably included letter names, occasionally the odd standard notation symbol, but never did he indicate duration or mood in this series of compositions. Then, a couple of months later, Joel began to notate

FIGURE 3–21 *An invented notation using letter names and (redundant) music symbols* (This figure appears in Upitis 1987b, p. 114.)

The child's invented notation:

The piece as it would appear in standard notation:

his compositions so that durations were indicated through text and circles to show which notes operated together as a figure (see Figure 3–23). Hence, the instruction under the first E ("You Go TOREST eRe" means "You got to rest here") indicated a long note. Similarly, the circled G, A, and G, along with the instruction "CWIC" (quick) indicated these notes were to be played more quickly. In fact, the last note of the figure is longer, but nevertheless seems short due to its relationship with the two notes preceding it—a figural notation in terms of the earlier discussion.

The example in Figure 3–24 shows how Joel combined letter names and icons for black notes to indicate **accidentals**. The title of the piece, *Vibrator*, also neatly captures the mood of the piece and even serves as **tempo** marking (fast). This notation, in fact, may even be classified as correct rather than transitional, for the piece can be accurately reconstructed from the notation, as long as one understands the system. The issue of whether a notation is transitional or correct is one of the discussions in the next section.

Correct—Standard

I mentioned earlier that when children's notations of their own compositions in the context of music teaching are considered, we

FIGURE 3-22 *Invented notation using only letter names (no rhythm information)*

The child's invented notation:

The piece as it would appear in standard notation:

see that children learn to use standard notational symbols in a standard and regulated way. Unlike spelling development, however, I am prepared to accept more than one correct form of music notation. For instance, what Davidson and Scripp (1988a) term regulated (Level 3) notation may well be seen as a form of correct notation, if it is successful in capturing the rhythmic and melodic elements of the melody so that the original composition can be performed from the notation.

At the correct stage of spelling development, children have a large body of words that they spell correctly, reflecting their knowledge of English orthography, and the basic rules thereof (Gentry 1982). The child can also think of alternate spellings for a given word when attempting to come up with the correct or standard spelling. The correct forms of music notation, whether with standard notation symbols or other symbols, are most notable for two features: the child understands the concept of absolute pitch including the relationship of **tones** and **semi-tones**, and the child is successful at notating rhythm in a metered way. An example of

FIGURE 3–23 *Invented notation using letter names for pitch, and words to indicate rhythm* (This figure appears in Upitis 1987b, p. 116.)

The child's invented notation:

The piece as it would appear in standard notation:

a correct notation, using standard music notation symbols, is given in Figure 3–25.[4]

Another example of what might be seen as a correct notation is given in Figure 3–26. Here the symbols are not standard music symbols, but if one knows the rules of the system, the piece can be reproduced. Interestingly, some of the computer programs using non-standard notation forms use a similar form to this for duration, where the length of the note is directly proportional to

---

[4]This notation was of the child's own composition, and was produced, four years later, by the same child whose music notations were shown in Figures 2–2 and 3–8.

FIGURE 3-24 *Using letter names and an icon for black notes to indicate accidentals,*
along with other symbols
(This figure appears in Upitis 1987b, p.117.)

The child's invented notation:

The piece as it would appear in standard notation:

the length of a rectangular bar (see Chapter 5). I would argue that this is another correct form of spelling a musical thought—correct, perhaps, in another language than the standard notation language we have traditionally regarded as *the* notation form for Western music.

Concluding Remarks

At the beginning of this chapter, I outlined a number of factors which likely affect a child's understanding of music notation. Two of those factors have been used in this chapter to describe the research on children's notation, namely music training and the development of invented notational systems. Some readers may have noticed that in the discussion of stages of development, I made no mention of the ages at which one might expect different

FIGURE 3-25 *Correct and standard music notation*

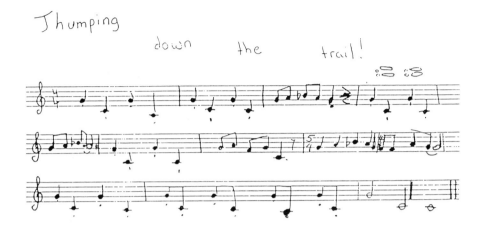

kinds of notations to be generated. The reason for this is simple. While the order of notational development appears to be predictable, children create notations of a given type at a wide variety of ages, presumably because music instruction is much less uniform than instruction in reading, writing, and spelling. So, while Davidson and Scripp (1988a) found that seven-year-olds could notate melodic contour, other researchers have found this kind of notation emerging at a later age (at nine years; Linton 1991). I have found that children as young as five years of age may notate melodic contour, if they are involved in composition, and as late as ten years of age if they are not. I am convinced that the ages are less important than the *nature* of the development that occurs when children begin to explore and use notation. Personal history begins when people begin to use and develop notations, whether at the age of five or twenty-five, and whether the notation is for music or for words.

And other factors? A discussion on the interaction between performance and notation is coming up. And, as time passes, I have become keenly interested in two more factors—the effects of the "home musical diet" on children's compositions and their notations, and the quality of the compositions themselves. What makes a good composition, as perceived by the child and the au-

FIGURE 3–26 *Correct and non-standard music notation*

The child's invented notation: the numbers indicate which fingers are to be used in playing the recorder; the length of the rectangular bar indicates the duration of the note (a metric system):

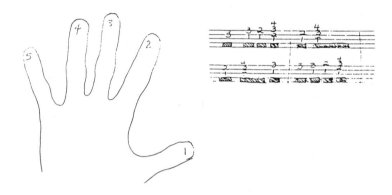

The piece as it would appear in standard notation:

dience? While I have yet to explore these issues at length, those who undertake this kind of work with children may well keep these ideas in mind. Then, when such notions as home diet and quality of music are considered seriously by other researchers and other teachers, we will have a template of ideas, stories, and experiences to share.

Interactions Between Performance and Notation

▲ ▲ ▲ ▲ ▲ ▲ ▲ ▲ ▲ ▲ ▲ ▲ ▲ ▲ ▲ ▲ ▲ ▲ THERE are many aspects of performance that affect the notation used by a child. They include such things as instrument choice, interactions with other children as a piece is performed for the first time, and more generally, the intertwining relationship among improvisation, notation, composition, and performance. Performance and composition, and therefore notation, are by their very nature linked, and remain linked long after a piece is "finished." In fact, one of the more unfortunate aspects of formal music training is the tendency to teach **harmony**, an integral part of composition, as something separate from the instrument. While this is changing in some contexts, it is not unusual to see conservatory students being taught the rules of harmony without an instrument in sight. I remember well learning music theory myself, and being told that I couldn't use the piano because that was "cheating." But I was also fortunate to have one teacher who realized that divorcing the instrument from the theory was fatal, and so, always taught with a keyboard at hand, and a record player by her side. In this chapter, it will be shown that learning the rules of harmony, and indeed, systematically developing one's own rules of composition, is not only possible with an instrument at hand, but possible in a much deeper way and at a much earlier age than one might think.

Instrument Choice

The first factor of performance affecting notation is the obvious one of instrument choice. If a child uses a drum, for example, he or she is unlikely to be concerned with notation for pitch, since most drums are primarily rhythm instruments. Likewise, though, if the child is improvising on the piano and eventually decides to notate the improvisation, then pitch is likely to be of primary importance, and rhythm secondary. In fact, when children first try to take account of pitch in their notations, it is not unusual for them to forget about rhythm altogether, returning to a "units" notation for rhythm (see Chapter 3). In any case, when considering the notational development patterns of children, the instrument used to make the notation is important. And, when working to extend the notations used by children, sometimes merely changing the instrument can be enough for a child to begin considering new dimensions of musical notation.

An example of a rather sophisticated notation for two tambourines appears in Figure 4–1. The two girls who notated this piece had a difficult time capturing the arm movements (shown by symbols like the star), going beyond notating the rhythm pattern

---

FIGURE 4–1 *A notation for two tambourines*

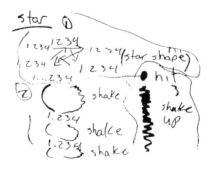

The invented notation:

The piece as it would appear in standard notation:

to a notation of choreography as well. An entirely different notation appears in Figure 4–2. This piece was written for an Orff metallophone, but might well have been written for another pitched instrument where letter names could be used, such as the piano notations of Joel that appear throughout the previous chapter. In fact, children often delight in trying out these pitch name notations not on the instrument for which they were composed, but on

Creating a Notation for a Non-pitched Rhythm Instrument

another instrument, comparing the effects of one to the other. This doesn't work as well for notations that are highly instrument dependent, like the tambourine example just described or the recorder notation pictured at the end of the last chapter (see Figure 3–26),

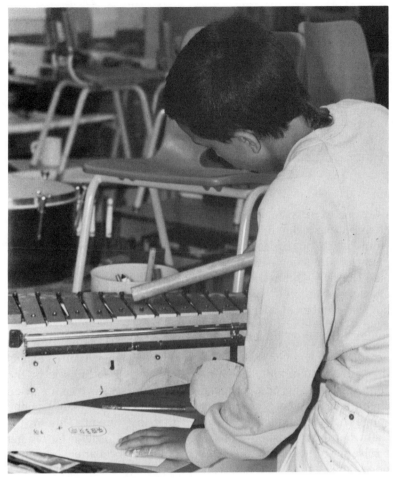

Creating a Notation for a Pitched Instrument

where the composer indicated which notes were to be played on
the recorder by naming the fingers covering the holes on the recorder. (I now wonder what might have happened had I asked the
child to notate the same piece for another instrument.)

Sometimes one's familiarity with an instrument means that
the notation is unsuccessful over time. An example is shown in
Figure 4–3. Here the child had played the piano for some time,
and had one day composed a piece for her cat, called *Kittens*. Her
notation was simply a sketch, enough, she thought, to play the
piece for me a week or so later. She noted with some dismay when

FIGURE 4–3 *An unsuccessful piano notation:* Kittens

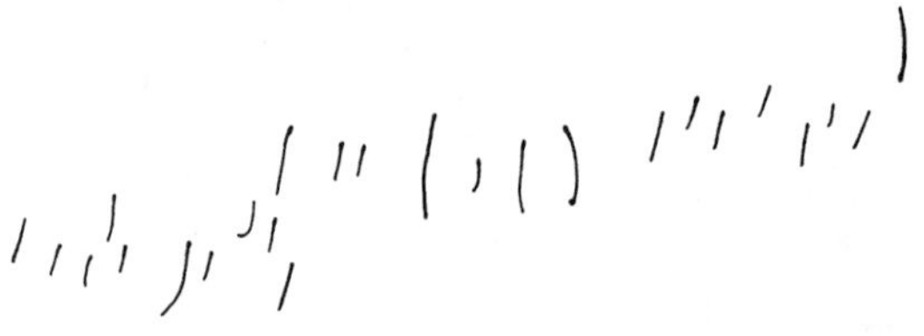

she came to play the piece that "I did *Kittens* and Mom really liked it, so I wrote it down but now I've totally forgotten it. I thought it would work, but I guess it didn't." A week later, she wrote another piece for the same cat called *Ode To Tailor*, with greater success (see Figure 4–4). She had no difficulty reading from this notation even a month later, having not only shown which notes to play, but the number of notes, the rhythm, and even the fingers to be used.

In some cases, the choice of instrument affects not only the notation but the very music that is notated. One instance of this that I have commonly encountered in school settings is in the context of playing and composing for recorders. Typically, when children begin composing for recorders, they like to notate the songs that are familiar to them for that instrument. This means that when I ask kids to "write something for recorder," I often get a class set of something like *Hot Cross Buns*. Soon after, however, once they realize that they can compose on what for them is a traditional instrument, they are likely to compose and notate highly original and often quite lovely melodies (see Figure 4–5). In the notation shown in Figure 4–5, the child has used letter names for pitches, and in this case, to her delight, I played her piece on the piano from her notation as well.

One of the other ways that an instrument affects composition is when the child is inspired by a particular instrument or performer. Just as well-known composers sometimes write for particular instrumentalists, so too do children find inspiration from the instruments they are exposed to and the performers they meet. A case-in-point occurred with a six-year-old child and an accomplished Hungarian 'cellist. Krysta had heard Katalin perform at a

FIGURE 4–4 *A successful piano notation:* Ode to Tailor

The invented notation:

The piece as it would appear in standard notation:

concert in my home, and was captivated by her persona and performance. At her next lesson, she told me that she wanted to "write a song for the lady in the red dress," and of course, I encouraged her to do so. What surprised us all, however, was the resulting work—a haunting melody that was ideal not only for the 'cello but for Katalin herself. I embellished the piano accompaniment slightly, building on the chord structure that Krysta had outlined. At the next soirée, Krysta's piece was performed by Katalin and myself, just as Krysta had envisaged, but could not herself play. This aspect of composition, namely writing music that is to be performed by

FIGURE 4–5 *An original recorder melody and notation*

The invented notation:

The piece as it would appear in standard notation:

others, makes the interaction between composition and performance even more complex, for in so doing, the child, while using
his or her own instrument to aid in the composition, needs to rely
on another performer or performers to hear the final result. Another example of such a composition is given in the next chapter,
where the composer wrote a piece for flute, clarinet, and piano.
However, to overcome the difficulties in imagining parts that she
could not herself play, a computer and synthesizer were used so
that all three parts could be played and modified both separately
and simultaneously.

Relationships Between Invented
and Standard Notations

Another form of interaction that arises out of performance is between invented notations and standard notational forms. As chil-

dren become more fluent both in their own notations and in standard notations, they begin to move back and forth between the two, acknowledging the times when, and the reasons for which, they prefer one form over another.

I have mentioned before that a child may find that his or her own notation is more difficult or awkward to use than standard notation. In some cases, this dissatisfaction is with respect to particular aspects of notation, for example, the notation of accidentals for a piano composition. At other times, an invented notation for an entire composition becomes so convoluted that the child will express the need for switching to a different form. An example of the latter appears in Figure 4–6. This is an early notation created by Krysta, the child who later wrote the piece for 'cello and piano discussed above. In this notation, Krysta had accounted for several aspects of the composition, including accidentals (marked by an "x"), **solid form** (indicated by a line under the notes to be played together), **octave** placement (*L* for lower octaves), and pitch. She commented:

> The *X*'s are there because they're all black notes. And I think they sound prettier than the white notes. They're kind of like bouncing on a balance beam with your fingers. . . . I did this while Mummy was still in bed . . . That line's there because you play these notes solid. All together, at the same time. I drew a line . . . I think yours [i.e. standard notation] is a little better for this.

On the other hand, sometimes it is not standard notation but an invented notation which is more appropriate. This is often the case when a child has been using letter names for pitches for some time in his or her own compositions, and then is faced with learning to read standard notation in order to play the compositions of others. This was the case for Ricky, Krysta's younger brother. It was close to Christmas, and Ricky had decided to learn *Good King Wenceslas*, which he had found in a book of carols. He had written out all of the pitches by letter name, an easier and therefore more accessible notation to him (see Figure 4–7). When I saw it, I asked him about it, and the following conversation took place:

RENA: What's this?
RICKY: That's *Old King Wenceslas*.
RENA: Why did you do this?
RICKY: It's the notes. See the other way it's hard. You have to know what all the notes are. And you don't have to help me. [Ricky then played from his notation.]

FIGURE 4-6 *A notation later translated to standard music notation*

The invented notation:

The piece as it later appeared in standard notation:

RENA: How did you do it? The writing I mean.
RICKY: I listened to Krysta, and I writed them. Now we'll try
   the hard one [played from standard notation].

Interestingly, when Ricky played *Good King Wenceslas* the second time, from standard notation rather than from his own, his
performance was much better. This may have been because he had
just played it, and the second time came easier. But it is more
likely, I think, that the standard notation was not completely foreign to him—he could see the shape of the piece, and because he
already knew the pitches to some extent, he could use the standard
notation for something beyond the notes alone.
   Music teachers may well recognize this phenomenon of children using note names to assist in the reading of standard notation,

FIGURE 4–7 *Letter names and standard notation for* Good King Wenceslas

Letter names:

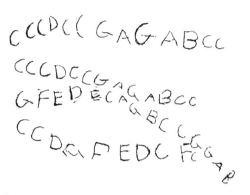

Standard notation:

whether they have been involved in composition or not. There is often some frustration, at least on the part of teachers, when they see children marking in note names, due in large part to the concern that if kids write in note names, then "they'll never learn to read." When I first began teaching children to play the piano, I felt the same way myself. But I have come to realize that whatever kids do to make sense of notation is more likely to be helpful than not. At least it is an attempt to understand the standard form and to translate that understanding to performance. And at best, as for

Ricky, it can be a way of extending a child's understanding of notation in general, relating one notational form to another. For it is always the case, as indicated even by the research on rhythm notation described in the previous chapter, that children can make sense of more than one notation at any given time. However, the context will dictate which notational forms they choose to use, both for reading someone else's work and for writing their own.

A completely different occurrence related to performance and notation sometimes happens when a child's notation is used by another person in performance, or when a child's improvisation is notated by someone else and then shown to the child. Many times I have noticed that the effect of performing a piece from a notation in one of these ways is that the child is more impressed by the notation than by the piece itself, as if they are realizing, for the first time, the profound power they have in using a symbol system. For example, when I had sketched down one of Joel's pieces, he asked to see what I had written. I showed him, explaining that it was his piece, and that I had written it down so that I could re-member it (thinking that some day I might be writing a book about all of this, and knowing that the stories would give it life). Joel, with obvious glee, stated, "That's how much notes I played and I didn't even know it? Is that supposed to be a Shakespeare thing?" For a while after that incident Joel would play long and intricate songs for me to notate, with the obvious underlying premise that the more, the better—and the more like Shakespeare. Similarly, when a child had developed a notation for water bottles, and found that I could play from it, she produced pages and pages filled with the same symbols (see Figure 4–8), caring not what the piece sounded like, but rather, producing a lengthy notation so that she might bid someone to play from her music. This idea of "writ[ing] something down and then see[ing] what it sounds like" is not uncommon once the relationship between the notation and per-formance becomes apparent. It is also my experience, however, that after a few of these notations are generated without the in-strument, the child soon enough returns to the instrument, writing a piece as it develops, rather than using the notation to develop the piece. In some cases, children achieve a balance of the two, trying some things in notation first, then playing on the instrument, and moving back to the notation again. This, however, tends to happen only after the child has some sense of the relationship between the notation and the overall form of a piece of music. For example, if a child has been in the practice of using an A–B–A

FIGURE 4–8 *Using symbols to generate performance.*

Piece for Water Bottle

FIGURE 4-9 *A composition created with patterns in mind*

form, where the beginning and ending sections are the same, but something different happens in the middle, then he or she would not necessarily need to play the last section before notating it, and may even make a few minor changes to the last section without consulting the instrument. This happens when children realize how highly patterned music can be—as the child who once told me, "Miss U! I've discovered your secret. I know how you compose. You just put together patterns of notes." The child who made this discovery then started to compose by pattern rather than by note, repeating sections, altering motifs by moving them up or down a fixed amount, and generally planning section by section rather than note by note (see Figure 4–9). In this case, she did not need to use her instrument for the entire process, but referred to the instrument when she wanted to work out a phrase, or see how a phrase might sound if it began a few notes lower. Throughout this process of composition and notation it was possible for me to make explicit various issues of form such as closure, repetition, tension and resolution, symmetry, and so on, in a way that is more difficult to do through improvisation alone, or through studying only the works of other composers.

While fluency with notation may enhance a child's understanding of pattern and form and thus enrich his or her compositions, as in the above example, there are also times when notation limits the work of the child. For instance, I have often heard children create elaborate improvisations, but because their notational skills lag behind their playing abilities, the compositions they eventually notate and perform are much simpler than their improvisations. This is not unlike stories that children tell as compared to stories that they write. While their oral renditions might be colorful and complex, their written stories are limited by the vocabulary they can generate on paper. In a similar way, what children are capable of reading is often of a higher level than what they write, whether they are reading and writing prose or music. Thus, once again, it is important to bear in mind that what is produced on paper may not necessarily reflect what the child can interpret through performance (reading text or music) or create through improvisation (storytelling or playing an instrument). While no-tation can be either paralyzing or enriching in a particular instance, it is also true that in the long run, an understanding of notation generally enhances one's abilities to make sense of the music of others and to write one's own, as does a growing fluency with written language.

Trends Over Time—Intervals, Scales, and Themes

One of the benefits of watching children develop notational sys-tems over a long period of time is that some intriguing trends begin to emerge. For example, after children have improvised on a num-ber of instruments in a variety of ways, generating notations and reading those of others, I have observed that they often become interested in defining **scales** and intervals, and systematically ex-ploring the possibilities of each. The interest in scales is often re-flected by children defining their own scales (see Figure 4–10). The interest in defining scales comes in part, no doubt, from the grow-ing understanding over time that most given pieces of tonal West-ern music are written from a fixed set of pitches forming the scale or key. Sometimes the scale is made explicit by an improvisation exercise that is instrument dependent (e.g., using the black keys on the piano, forming a pentatonic scale). After learning about some keys in these ways, that is, through improvisation, compo-sition and performing from notation, it makes sense that children would want to define their own scales. Once they have done so, they often write in their "key," exploring the ways that the notes of their scale can be combined.

A related interest is that of intervals. After playing a keyboard instrument for some time, it is common for children to identify intervals that sound pleasing to them, and then using those inter-

FIGURE 4–10 *A child's scale*

A piece written with scale passages:
(This figure appears in *This Too Is Music*: Upitis 1990b, p. 71.)

The piece as it would appear in standard notation:

Kangaroo

Allegretto

vals as inspiration for compositions. Typically, the interval of a third is used in this way (see Figure 4–11). Thus, the child may experiment with broken thirds (two notes played separately) or solid thirds (two notes played at once), and often will move up and down a scale using the interval. After playing around with thirds in this way, some children try other intervals as well (see Figure 4–12), writing pieces for each interval. In later compositions, while children may not base an entire piece on a given interval, they often write a section using a device they developed when first playing around with the notions of interval or scale.

FIGURE 4–11 *Pieces based on thirds*
        (*Bird* and *Panda Bear* appear in *This Too Is Music*: Upitis 1990b, on
        pages 65 & 71, respectively).

continued on next page

FIGURE 4–11 *continued from previous page*

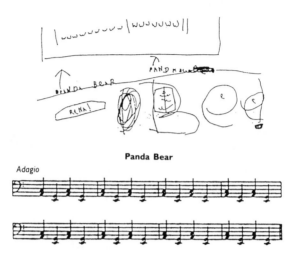

Panda Bear

Adagio

Another trend that can be observed over time is children's interest in writing around a given theme, and eventually, a style of composition that becomes characteristic of the child. Beatrice was always interested in animals, and particularly in rabbits. She wrote many compositions for rabbits and bunnies (see Figure 4–13), and in so doing, experimented extensively with staccato sounds (a detached style of playing, creating a light or hopping sound), and became interested in using fifths, especially in the accompanying left-hand chords. The interest in using fifths carried over to her other works as well, contributing to the overall effect of her compositions that brands them as distinctively her own. Just as Mozart sounds like Mozart, and Chopin sounds like Chopin, Beatrice sounds like Beatrice. Each piece is different, but nevertheless, there are features that make it possible to identify her writing.

Performing With Others—
Instruments, Notation, and Harmony

I think the most amazing and probably the most gratifying moments that come in working with children's music making are those

FIGURE 4–12 *Pieces based on thirds, fourths, and fifths*

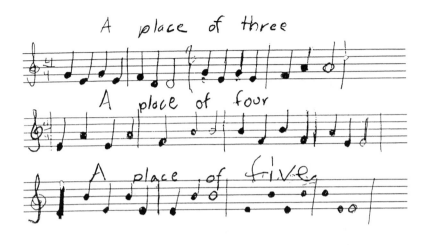

times when children come to understand some of the deeper aspects of composition, performance, and notation as a result of their own explorations, and explorations that they navigate with the people in their immediate vicinity.

About a year ago, a colleague who is a teacher, parent, and musician, described at length an exploration that was guided by his daughter Beth. He wrote:

> At supper time, Beth (6 years 3 months) was singing with obvious joy a color song she had learned at school from her French teacher [see Figure 4–14]. . . . She taught me the song, which took me several tries and some fumbling. We were both pleased when I finally got it. When I suggested she not move her head so much, she mentioned that the music felt that way, up and down, which she illustrated. I suggested she use her whole body, so she walked the song as she sang it. This was the beginning of walking the song which we did many times later on.
>
> She then returned to her place at the table facing . . . the refrigerator. In a moment of insight, she went quickly to the refrigerator, grabbed three yellow letters, arranged them in a row as she sang in slow motion, added a blue, then two groups of two reds. This represented half the song. She then reused the yellows for the second half, and got three more blues to make

FIGURE 4–13 *Rabbit compositions*

At five years (the standard notation is not available; this was composed at around the same time as *Bird*, *Panda Bear*, and *Kangaroo*, which appear earlier in this chapter):

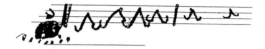

At six years:

At nine years (the original handwritten version of this piece appears in Figure 3–25; the composer later transcribed the melody and added a left-hand accompaniment on the computer):

up the second ending. I suggested she set the first ending (two reds) a little higher and the three blues a little lower, and demonstrated by pointing as I sang the song. She had a different solution: keep the reds in line until they have to be moved; move them away quickly and slide the blues into place (from below) just in time for the second ending.

She then went off to her room upstairs. Above the kitchen, we could hear her vigorous scratching on the floor. We hoped it was all on paper. In a few minutes Beth returned with a pile of papers, one corresponding to each of the plastic letters she had used earlier. The first three sheets had yellow suns in the middle. There followed a blue, four reds, and three blues . . . She laid them out on the floor in the same pattern as she had used on the refrigerator.

As we took turns "walking" the song, we became acutely aware of the problem of having to dash back to start the second half of the song. I could not resist suggesting that Beth put the papers in a circle. . . . She laid out the papers with the two endings interleaved: blue-red-blue-red-blue.

I then suggested Beth play the song on the piano. Several times while getting started at this, she said she could not do it, but a little encouragement kept her going. Eventually I received an excited call that she was ready, and I taped her performance. . . .

The whole session was a great pleasure for both of us. The roles of learning, teaching, and inventing were shared sensitively between us. For me it was an opportunity to make music with my own child, to watch mind and spirit at work, and to collaborate in learning . . . Every aspect of recording and playing music was represented: performing with voice and body, inventing and re-

FIGURE 4–14 *The Color Song*

fining notation, and learning, practicing, and performing on another instrument. (Egnatoff 1989)

Here, then, is an example of how a child began with a song
she had heard in another context, developed more than one notation for it (with the fridge magnets, movement, and pieces of
paper), and ultimately, taught it to someone else and learned to
play it on another instrument. Here the issues of notation are so
intricately interwoven with performance that they are virtually inseparable. But in the hour or so over which the described events
took place, not only did Beth come to understand the form of the
piece through the notation she developed, but managed to convey
that understanding to her father as well.

Another instance where family members strongly influenced
each other during a music making session occurred between Ricky
and Krysta, the brother and sister described earlier. Both children
were learning to play the piano, with considerable emphasis on
improvisation and composition as part of the process. We will never
know the sequence of events leading to the duet composed by
Ricky and Krysta (see Figure 4–15) for there was no one to record
the incident as was the case for the work between Beth and her
father. But somehow the two children, at that time four and six
years old, put together a duet, which they played with great pride
for me and for their parents. I notated the piece after hearing them
play it several times. Krysta then laboriously read her part from
my notation, partly to check that I had it right, and partly to ex-

FIGURE 4–15 *A Duet*

Krysta's part:

Ricky's part (played two octaves higher than written):

FIGURE 4–16 *A notation showing the tonic key*

The invented notation:

The piece as it would appear in standard notation:

(The rhythm of the piece cannot be discerned from the notation, but was consistently played by the child in the manner indicated. As mentioned in the text, the solid left side of the heart isn't to be played — it merely indicates the tonality of the piece, while the stripes on the right side, read top to bottom, indicate the individual pitches.)

perience the satisfaction of reading her part from notation—notation more complex than she was reading in her pieces, but one that she was nevertheless motivated and able to play because it was a notation of her own composition.

I have one last example to describe before bringing this chapter to a close. One of my favorite notations is pictured in Figure 4–16. This was produced by Ricky, to represent a composition he created at the age of four. The bands of color on the right side of the heart indicated the notes to be played. At first glance, this appeared to be a relatively simple notation, where each band represented a different note, and one played the piece from top to bottom. Naturally, I asked Ricky why he had colored the left side of the heart black, the same color used for the note C on the other side of the heart, which was also the key of the piece. He looked at me solemnly. "Listen," he said, and played the piece again, holding his ear close to the keys. He then looked up at me expectantly. I had no idea what he was trying to convey, and listened again as he played once more. Finally, he turned to me, and, referring to the left side of the heart, opened his arms and said, "It says *ALL*." And indeed it does. For it is in relation to the tonic or home note, in this case C, that all other notes take their identity. C *is* all. And so, Ricky demonstrated to me in a way that I will never forget that he could not only invent a notation for his piece, but that he also understood and could convey the underlying tonality. He did not need to have this concept taught to him as discrete fact of music theory. Rather, it was something that he could develop directly from the instrument that he played.

Enhancing Children's Invented Notations

▲ ▲ ▲ ▲ ▲ ▲ ▲ ▲ ▲ ▲ ▲ ▲ ▲ ▲ ▲ ▲ ▲ ▲ ▲   IF we recognize that children's notations are a way of making meaning of music and of communicating that meaning to others, then as teachers one of our gifts to children should be that of helping them develop better ways of conveying meaning. In the previous chapters, I have shown how incredibly complex children's notations can be, and how they are influenced by performance, instruments, and the people with whom the notations are shared. In this chapter, I am going to outline specific possibilities for extending the very meaningful use of symbols that children offer.

There are three ways in which I will pursue the issue of enhancing children's invented notations. The first is a series of general principles of interacting with children as they develop notations, ways of adding more to their repertoire of symbols that is in some sense congruent with their notational development. The second section is a description of a series of activities, designed for the classroom, which serve to build on what children already know about notation—lessons, if you will. The final section is a detailed discussion of how the computer might be used as a specific tool in meeting some of the general principles and specific lessons considered.

General Ways of Enhancing Notations

In the second chapter of this book, I described a whole host of things that parents could do at home, and teachers could do in and out of school, to make children's music environments richer. But when we provide richer environments where children start generating and sharing notations, how do we help this process flourish? I will describe a few techniques here, including (1) developing the notation system used by the child, (2) introducing standard notation when an invented notation becomes too cumbersome, (3) continually reinforcing the idea that there are many ways to notate the same piece of music, and (4) emphasizing various issues and practices that are also considered important in a process writing approach, such as considering the audience, keeping writing folders, conferencing, and teaching about specific aspects of musical grammar as the need arises from the children's own works.

Perhaps the most important approach to bear in mind when thinking about enhancing children's invented notations, is to help them develop the particular system they choose to use, at the level at which they are using it. Just as Gentry (1982) argues that there is little point teaching phonetic spelling rules when the child is at, say, the precommunicative stage of spelling, it also makes little sense to try to introduce a system of regulated pitches when the child is more interested in encoding the number of events. But, when a child is using invented systems that capture melodic contour, it makes perfect sense to talk about the shape of a melody, and to show the child different ways in which contour might be notated.

Within a given system, a child will, over time, develop more features to account for more information as he or she moves in some way through the stages of notational development outlined in Chapters 3 and 4. I have indicated that for some children, the system might be graphic, for others, numeric, and for others, an alphabetic system or a combination of various systems. Joel, for example, used an alphabetic system for quite a while, using letter names for pitches, and then modifying the system until it could be used to deal with the complexities of rhythm as well (see Figure 3–23). It matters little, however, what kind of system a child chooses to use. Each can be developed to include all sorts of music information.

Sometimes as a system evolves, it become too cumbersome to read. In an attempt to notate everything about a melody—pitch, rhythm, dynamics, tempo, and so on—the system is developed to death. One of the notations shown in the first chapter (see Figure 1–7) falls under this category. The notation is primarily a numeric system, where the reader finds each pitch relative to the last by counting up or down as indicated by the notation. By the time the child had produced this notation, he had developed it far enough to deal with rhythm as well, by using slurs to show the length of the notes. While this notation is certainly sophisticated and includes a good deal of melodic information, it is nevertheless the kind of notation that one could get lost with—like directions to someone's house that are made up of left and right turns. If you make one wrong turn, everything else from then on in is also wrong. This notation shares that problem—if the reader doesn't go down or up the right number of keys, all of the subsequent notes will be wrong as well. The direction "always end on A♯ (G♭)" is a bit like saying "If you get to the big oak tree, you've gone too far." That is, if the reader of this notation ends on some note other than A♯, a mistake has been made somewhere along the line. When William finished with this notation, he realized that he had captured his piece just the way he played it, but he was not surprised at my dismay at having to try to read it. With a bit of a sigh and a grin, he told me, "It's a hard one." At this point, it made sense to translate his notation into standard notation, for in fact, standard notation was easier to read than the notation William had developed—even for William. But the development of his own notation was not a waste of William's time, nor of mine. Even though the notation proved too complex to use in the long run, by developing the notation, he came to understand better the elements of melody that one tries to capture in using a notation system. He also came to understand how his notation differed from standard notation, and more generally, how different systems might be used to encode the same information.

In the previous chapters, I have also described how children develop fluency with more than one form of notation. Even the early rather narrowly defined studies on rhythm notation indicated that most children could read and write both figural and metric notations. How then can this understanding of different forms be enhanced? One way, of course, is to simply have children share their notations with each other—a practice I have used for many years. Thus, in addition to sharing compositions through performance, we should encourage children to share the notations as well. In this way, children not only become more tolerant of forms that are different from theirs, but may also learn something about other notation techniques. This can, of course, be extended to examining notations made by other composers—such as the notations of a twentieth-century composer reproduced in the first chapter (see Figure 1–10). Add to this the notations used over the past four or five centuries, in secular and sacred music of many cultures, and children will undoubtedly come to see their own work as part of a colorful history and developing future.

Another thought to keep in mind when encouraging notational development is that one should be aware of the child's thoughts about his or her intended audience. Given what we know about some children's concern—or lack of it—for the reader of the notations they develop, it also makes sense to discuss with children the knowledge of the reader for whom they are writing. Will the person be able to interpret the symbols without ambiguity? Recall the discussion in Chapter 3 about Joel's absolute certainty that his notation would only be read by people he knew, people to whom he could explain the system, should any questions arise. This issue of audience, like so many of the general issues discussed here, is one that is important for the writing of prose as well.

Another practice I have adopted from proponents of the whole language/process writing approach is the use of writing folders. By providing children with a folder for their compositions, with pockets for completed work and work in progress, children and teachers can monitor their writing development just as they would with the writing of text. Thus, children are encouraged to work on pieces over a period of time, coming back to some pieces for revision, editing, and ultimately for publication and performance.

A further hallmark of a whole language approach to writing and reading is the notion of conferencing, where children have a chance to confer with their teacher and/or their peers about their work in progress. This allows the teacher to determine many things, including specific needs or weaknesses a child might have, as indicated in the writing itself. In the case of music, after a series of conferences, I might find that a whole group of children are using different invented symbols for a specific function, such as the **glissando**. I would then pull those children aside for a few minutes, have them compare their notations, and introduce the

Editing a Composition from a Writing Folder

standard Italian term. Having done this, I would expect to see it emerge in their writing, and even in the writing of other children in the group, who learned the term from someone attending the conference. Some examples of other terms, notational symbols, and skills that can be found and shaped in this way are discussed in the following section.

Specific Notation Activities

I have already described a specific activity, namely, introducing standard symbols as children begin to use invented symbols for the same function consistently. Interestingly, children appear to be much more concerned with such things as showing repetition, the end of the piece, the clef, dynamics (although they often confuse loud and fast, and similarly, soft and slow), and special effects of some type (like the glissando or **pizzicato**) than in notating rhythm and pitch in some systematic way. This makes me ask, once again, why we bother teaching pitch and rhythm first, if children regard pitch and rhythm as less important characteristics, even in their own music.

FIGURE 5–1 *Using a STOP sign to show the end of the piece*

I have found that the first standard notation symbols that children ask for, or are willing to hear about, typically include the treble clef, the repeat sign, the double barline, accents, the glissando, soon after followed by a concern about dynamics, special notes such as accidentals, and possibly tempo. For example, in the notation appearing in Figure 5–1, the child has used a stop sign to indicate the end of the piece. At this point, it makes good sense to show another way of notating the end, that is, the double barline. Similarly, the child using a "pirate's knife" to signify F♯, as shown in Figure 5–2, is much more likely to be interested in the standard sign for a **sharp** (♯), having developed a symbol for the function already, than a child who is composing pieces on white notes only.

Another example is given in Figure 5–3. Here, the child had already adapted some standard symbols in his invented system, and when I approached him, he knew that I would be offering another way of notating "the end." We had the following conversation:

LYLE: How do they do it?
RENA: Like this. With a double barline.
LYLE: Oh. Are you a vegetarian?
RENA: Yes.
LYLE: So is my mother.
(Conversations like these seldom end with the notational issue at hand. I sometimes think that kids are trying to figure out just what role I am playing when I tell them something about standard notation. Am I a teacher? A friend? A vegetarian? A Martian?)

There comes a time, of course, when it makes sense to teach children something about standard notation for pitch and rhythm as well. I usually start with rhythm, since many of their compo-

FIGURE 5-2 *Using a knife to indicate a sharp* (♯)
      (This figure appears in *This Too Is Music*: Upitis 1990b, p.63.)

The invented notation:

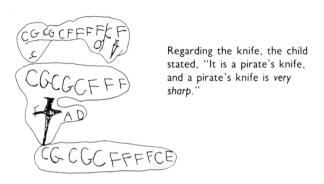

Regarding the knife, the child stated, "It is a pirate's knife, and a pirate's knife is *very sharp.*"

The piece as it would appear in standard notation:

sitions are for rhythm instruments like the tambourine, and thus, pitch doesn't come into the picture until later. But it's also usually easier to teach rhythm, especially if one takes into account the kinds of research findings outlined in Chapter 3, namely that kids respond to rhythm in figural and metric ways, and that they dem-

FIGURE 5-3 *Incorporating the double barline*

The original notation:

The notation with a double barline:

onstrate their understanding not only in the notations that they read and create, but also in their motor responses. Thus, in teaching standard rhythm notation, one should somehow incorporate these things. I have developed several ways of doing so, and other teachers use complementary ideas. A few are now described.

Before even thinking about teaching standard rhythm notation, I spend a good deal of time having the children walk, run, and slide in response to the music I play. As time goes on, I indicate how walking notes are notated (quarter notes), and similarly, for running notes (eighth note pairs), and the slide (half notes). Sometimes I also have a small group of children measure durations by walking along the floor, side by side, so that they begin and end at the same time, but take different numbers of steps (e.g., two,

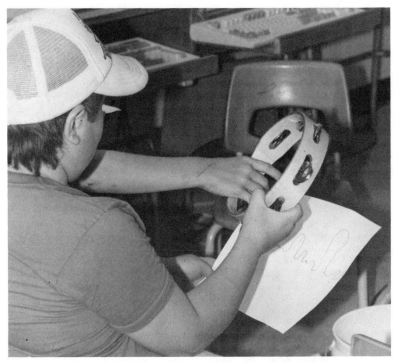

Composing a Piece for Tambourine Using an Invented Notation for Rhythm

four, eight, and sixteen steps). This can then be translated to standard durations, where the quarter notes are walked by the person taking eight steps, the eighth notes by the person taking sixteen steps, the half notes by the person taking four steps, and the whole notes by the person taking only two steps (see Figure 5–4). A similar exercise can be done with balls, where children bounce balls in the same ratios—1:2:4:8. This is a common Dalcroze exercise, yet another way that children can feel relative durations (see Dalcroze 1912, 1921).

Another way of teaching standard rhythm notation is through a kind of dictation exercise. Rather than the traditional dictation exercise, where the teacher claps or taps a pattern in the air, then asking the children to notate it, I play a pattern on a series of colored cards, where each card represents a beat. The kids have the same set of colored cards in front of them. Thus, in 4/4 or common time, there would be four cards, say a blue one, red one, green one, and yellow one, where each card is worth a quarter

Using Balls for Bouncing Different Durations

note. I then tap a simple pattern, made up of quarter (walking) and eighth (running) notes. Quarter notes translate to one tap on a card, eighth notes to two. Thus, a pattern of quarter, quarter, eighth-eighth, quarter (i.e., long, long, short-short, long, where each of the four beats is equal) would be played as one tap on the blue, one on the red, two on the green, and one on the yellow. After I finish tapping the pattern, I ask the kids to tap it back on their cards. In this way, they not only hear the pattern, they also see it—there's a sort of visual trace left over after the clapping is finished. This gives them three representations of the rhythm sequence—aural, visual, and kinesthetic. I am sure that by offering multiple representations of the same pattern, there is a far greater chance that the rhythm sequence will somehow make sense than if the pattern was presented in only one form.

I then ask the children to tell me about the pattern, with questions like, "What happened on red?" "Which card had running notes?" and other similar questions. I tap lots of patterns, and have them tap lots of patterns for each other. Then, I ask them to write the pattern using standard notation symbols. Since they "see" the pattern in a metric way, their notations are almost always metric.

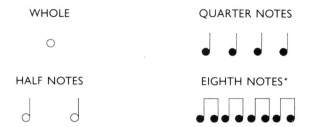

WHOLE   QUARTER NOTES

HALF NOTES   EIGHTH NOTES*

*Eighth notes, in this context, are usually represented as a pair by joining the stems across the top, indicating the value equivalent to a quarter note.

Notes and Rests

WHOLE   QUARTER

HALF   EIGHTH

That is, even though they might respond figurally if the pattern was clapped in the air, they respond metrically if they see the pattern laid out on the cards. In fact, I often do both, so that they can see for themselves the difference between a figural and metric notation. I have used this system to introduce all kinds of durations—quarters, eighths, dotted quarters, dotted halves, half notes, whole notes, triplets, and the corresponding rests. Also, I have many a time seen children trying to work out the rhythm sequence of a composition of their own by using the colored cards, or simply tapping the pattern spatially, left to right, on the floor or table.

I don't feel that there is a need, however, to feel or see all of the possible durations in the ways described above. While some music teaching approaches include ways of introducing other durations besides the simple ones I have described, I usually find that if children feel some, they can grasp the sense of others, even if taught in a more conventional and abstract way.

Tapping Rhythm Patterns in 4/4 Time Using a Card for Each Beat

How to teach standard pitch notation? As always, the need for standard notation should come from the children's own work. Sometimes this need is clear, as in the instance when a child develops a sophisticated but too complex system of his or her own, such as the one described earlier in this chapter. Sometimes, however, children will ask about pitch notation simply because they become curious about how it works. This is likely to happen if they have been exposed to different forms of notation, or in other ways have been sensitized to the issues of notational systems. In this vein, I have often had children ask me "How do you do it in notes?" when they have become curious in this way. In fact, they often ask to have a known melody notated, rather than their own. At first, I would find it incredibly odd to have kids ask me, time and time again, to show them how to notate something like *Hot Cross Buns* or *Twinkle, Twinkle, Little Star* in standard notation, especially when their own compositions were much more interesting and complex, or when the question came from a twelve-year-old on the verge of adolescence (I mean, really, why *Hot Cross Buns* of all things?). The answer, in part, is that these melodies are so familiar to children as real melodies, ones that they have known from childhood and even played on instruments themselves, that seeing them notated in standard notation somehow makes the notation

Standard notation for *Twinkle, Twinkle, Little Star*

The "made up" song, and the child's conversion of that song to standard notation:

more real as well. Once they see a familiar melody notated in this way, children often begin translating their own compositions to standard notation. When Hollie asked to see *Twinkle, Twinkle, Little Star* in standard notation, it didn't surprise me to see her showing it to everyone else in sight, watching the others copy her notation, and then "changing [her] made up song to notes," thereby making it more real as well (see Figure 5-5). Other teachers have commented on how eager kids seem to be to learn standard notation in this context, and not only eager, but quick in grasping the system. But why not? Children can learn to read text quickly as well, if they have an interest and enough related language background to do so.

The last series of specific suggestions I am going to describe in this chapter deal with composition exercises that I have used

Drawing in Response to a Piece of Music

over the years to augment the compositions made by children of their own accord. I will describe five such activities, roughly in order of difficulty, although there is no reason to present these ideas to children in this order if their work and interest indicates a different approach.

Listening and Drawing

One of the most dreary "music appreciation" exercises that has become commonplace over the past few years is that of listening to a piece of music, and drawing in response to it. Children of various ages usually like this activity the first time, but unless the activity is in some way extended, it quickly loses its appeal. One way of extending the activity is to show children how their drawings reflect a musical dimension, such as contour, relating their free form drawing to their invented notations. Another is to suggest to children that they might adapt some of the symbols they made while listening to their own notational systems for their compositions (see Figure 5–6). A third might be to take this exercise

FIGURE 5–6 *Adapting symbols from a listening and drawing exercise*

Free-form drawing
(in response to J.S. Bach's Two-Part Invention in F major):

Subsequent composition incorporating ideas from the earlier drawing:

The piece as it would appear in standard notation:

beyond music entirely, using a part of the drawing as the basis for a piece of artwork. Finally, children might find more meaning in the activity if they did it at long but fairly regular intervals, comparing how their drawings changed year by year.

Composing from Improvisations

While it would be an extensive task to try to outline the many different forms of improvisation that teachers might use, both for the sake of improvisation alone and to encourage composition, I will nevertheless outline a few. Some are described in more detail in another context (Upitis 1990b).

One of the first improvisation exercises I use with keyboard students is based on a pentatonic scale. One example of a pentatonic scale is the black notes. By playing the black notes in almost any combination, a huge variety of pleasing sounds can be produced. A pentatonic scale can be played on Orff instruments as well, by removing the notes that don't belong in the scale (e.g., C, D, F, G, and A make up another pentatonic scale). In fact, those teachers using an Orff or Kodaly approach to teaching music frequently make use of pentatonic keys, both for improvisation and for simple song repertoire.

When I have kids improvise on the pentatonic scale, I often make suggestions to give the improvisation some shape and direction. These suggestions can take the form of activity cards, especially if there are many children involved (see Figure 5–7). For example, when asked to depict different kinds of weather sounds, children might experiment with light, single, falling notes for rain, and loud bunches of low notes for thunder. Similarly, if I ask children to try making sounds to reflect different colors—"How would red sound?" "Yellow?" "Black?"—children then focus on different parts of the keyboard and with different dynamic levels. Finally, in an improvisation depicting a conversation between two people, such as a mother and a daughter arguing about what time the daughter should come home on a Friday night, the two players, mother and daughter, might make use of various musical devices—tempo, dynamics, texture, rhythm, and pitch, with the mother playing at the low end of the keyboard, and the daughter playing above. From these improvisations, children may then move into composing a more formal work, notating the result. This work may be quite removed from the earlier improvisation (e.g., a color improvisation) if it was created by developing some interesting sequence or effect through the improvisation itself.

In a similar way, improvisations based on other scales can lead to the development of compositions and notations. Another scale that I have used with great success is the G **major** scale with an F natural instead of F♯. By using a natural 7th note, many of the harmonic and melodic difficulties in working with a major key

FIGURE 5-7 *Activity cards for pentatonic improvisations*

> TRY MAKING SOUNDS FOR DIFFERENT KINDS
> OF WEATHER . . . WHAT WOULD A SUNNY
> DAY SOUND LIKE? RAIN? THUNDER?
> LIGHTNING?

> TRY MAKING SOUNDS FOR DIFFERENT COLORS.
> WHAT DOES YELLOW SOUND LIKE?
> HOW ABOUT RED? PURPLE? BLUE?
> WHAT HAPPENS IF YOU TRY PLAYING LOWER?
> HIGHER? WITH DIFFERENT INSTRUMENTS?

> TRY HAVING A CONVERSATION WITH A
> FRIEND. DECIDE FIRST OF ALL WHAT ROLE
> EACH OF YOU IS GOING TO PLAY. YOU MIGHT
> TRY SOMETHING LIKE . . .
>
> - A MOTHER AND A DAUGHTER
> - A USED CAR SALESMAN AND A BUYER
> - A TEACHER AND A STUDENT

disappear, and as with the pentatonic scale, children can improvise freely without being concerned about hitting the "right" notes. When engaged in this particular improvisation, I often play a simple bass as the child improvises above, or have another child or parent play the bass part (see Figure 5–8). Then, the child is encouraged to improvise above, using scale passages, the odd chord (particularly thirds), and many repeated notes. The results are often very beautiful. And children know that the sounds they are pro-

Improvising on the Keyboard Using a Natural Major Scale

ducing are good. As Hilary, who was five years old at the time, said, "This is good! I want to do this until I'm seven!"

A similar scale can be used in the **minor** mode. The key of A minor is also all white keys on the keyboard, which makes it easier for beginning players (see Figure 5–8). The D **natural minor** has a special quality, with one black key (B♭; again, see Figure 5–8). Two examples of contrasting pieces written in D natural minor appear in Figure 5–9.

Soundscapes

Soundscapes, like landscapes, are vast and impressive. I use the term soundscape to refer both to the huge, highly visual notations generated by this activity, and to the music itself. Soundscapes are often associated with Canadian composer Murray Schafer (Schafer 1975), and indeed, are a creature of his invention.

When making soundscapes with a group of children, I usually begin by mounting a large piece of mural paper on the wall (at least ten feet long), at a level that can be easily reached by the kids. I have available a variety of instruments, and markers, crayons, scraps of paper, and bits of "junk"—like bottle caps, icicles, stickers, and straws. On another piece of smaller paper, I draw a soundscape, for voices only, using vowels and sounds, and perhaps a word or two (see Figure 5–10). We then perform the soundscape,

FIGURE 5–8 *G natural major, and A and D natural minor keys*

G natural major

A natural minor

D natural minor

splitting into two or three groups as indicated by the notation, and adding dynamics as the piece demands. Thereafter, I initiate some discussion about the other available instruments—the kinds of sounds they make, how they contrast to one another, how voice effects could be used, which instruments might best be used for special effects, background rhythm, and so on. I then invite the children to think about what instruments they would like to play, and at what point in the composition. As they begin to try out various combinations, they start to come to some agreement about aspects of the composition, and when ready, notate their intentions on the mural paper (see Figure 5–11). For instance, a child may begin by suggesting that someone beat a drum throughout the piece. He or she would then be encouraged to make some notation to indicate that the drum is to play throughout, including the rhythm, the intensity, and any other dimension of the drumming seen as important.

When I do this activity with a full class of children, I usually divide them into four or five groups of about six children in each group, and ask that they not only notate an instrument for each of them to play, but also a part or two where the whole class can participate in the soundscape as it is performed (either clapped,

FIGURE 5–9 *Two contrasting compositions based on a D natural minor improvisation*

Happy and Sad

Untitled

FIGURE 5-10   *A Soundscape for voices*

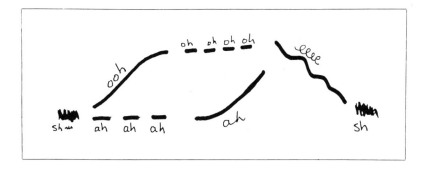

tapped, or sung parts). Sometimes the children will add new parts after they first hear it, sometimes not. Recording the performances is usually a good idea—a soundscape sounds very different when played from a tape recorder than when performed live. The final notations are as colorful as the pieces themselves—with icicles hanging off to indicate tambourines shaking, swooping colorful lines indicating similarly swooping voices, and strong even lines showing the beat of the drum.

Composing from a Conference Theme and Other Classroom Contexts

Often as children are working on compositions, there are opportunities to incorporate their music writing with other themes of study or special interest. For instance, a Grade 4 class, when faced with writing a book report on a novel they had recently read, suggested to their teacher that they write a group ballad instead of book reports. With all of the verses in the ballad, they were able to describe the features of the book (setting, characters, themes, and so on) that they would normally cover in their individual book reports. In another case, a group of children wrote a ballad to summarize a Social Studies unit on colonial times. In yet another case, a class decided to write songs, in groups of about four or five in each, on two themes—sports and the environment. In some cases, the song writing involved composing new lyrics to a familiar

FIGURE 5–11 *A Soundscape produced by a group of children*

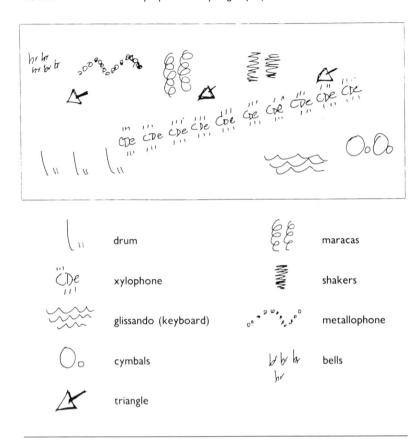

drum		maracas	
xylophone		shakers	
glissando (keyboard)		metallophone	
cymbals		bells	
triangle			

melody (see Figure 5–12). In others, children came up with both melody and words (see Figure 5–13).

Another kind of writing that emerges from conferences with children about their compositions is more specifically related to the music itself. For example, a few years ago a number of children became interested in writing rounds. A couple of children had tried to write a round with minimal success, another child had tried to play *Twinkle, Twinkle, Little Star* as a round on the computer and found that it didn't work (although the result was certainly interesting, and oddly appealing to some of us in the room). I pulled

FIGURE 5–12 *New words for a familiar melody*

Children's words:

Land of the Hockey Puck

(sung to the tune of *Land of the Silver Birch*)

Land of the Hockey King,
Home of the Gretsky
Where still Gordie Howe
Plays at will—

Swift as a Hockey King
Skates like a cheetah,
My mighty skates,
Carry me forth—

(Chorus)   Mom and Dad,
I will return again,
After the game, after the game,
After the game, game, game.

(Chorus)   Mom and Dad,
I will return again,
After the game, after the game,
After the game, game, game.

Original melody:

this group of children aside, and in a few minutes, by example and a brief explanation, related to them the harmonic rule for writing a round, namely that most of the notes had to belong to one chord. This concept of notes belonging to a chord was already familiar to the children in the group, based on their earlier improvisations and song writing. Not long after, many of them wrote their own rounds, which the class performed. An example is given in Figure 5–14.

FIGURE 5-13 *Group song writing*

An early draft:

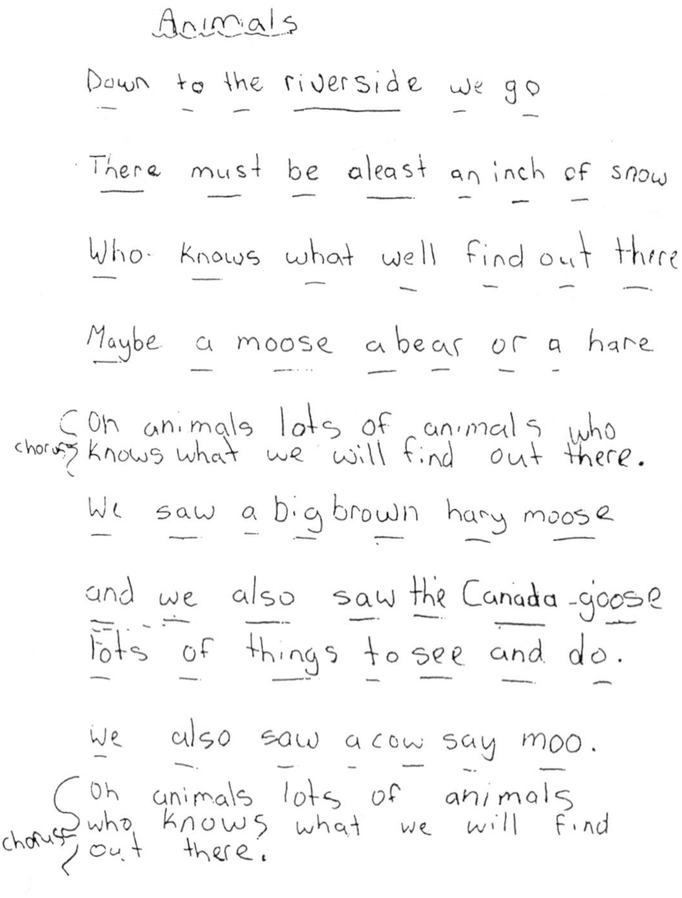

Animals

Down to the riverside we go

There must be aleast an inch of snow

Who. Knows what well find out there

Maybe a moose a bear or a hare

chorus { Oh animals lots of animals who
knows what we will find out there.

We saw a big brown hary moose

and we also saw the Canada -goose
lots of things to see and do.

We also saw a cow say moo.

chorus { Oh animals lots of animals
who knows what we will find
out there.

continued on next page

Composing by Form

This is an extension of the activities described above, where the
writing is directed not by theme or from something arising from
the children's explorations, but by a form introduced by a teacher.
The form can be either numerical in some sense, or based on a
particular musical idiom. I will give an example of both.

FIGURE 5–13   *continued from previous page*

The final printed copy:

Canadian Animals

We all love our cats, cats, cats
Especially catching rats, rats, rats.
Cats are cute, cats are cuddly,
Even when they're mud, mud, muddly.

(Chorus)   We all love our Canadian animals, animals, animals.

We all love our horse, horse, horses,
Especially when they're running course, course, courses.
Horses are big, horses are strong,
So go ride your horse before it is gone.

(Chorus)   We all love our Canadian animals, animals, animals.

We all love our moose, moose, mooses,
Especially when they're playing with goose, goose, gooses.
Mooses are huge, mooses are rouge,
It has no urges for eating goose, goose, gooses.

(Chorus)   We all love our Canadian animals, animals, animals.

We all love our mouse, mouse, mices,
Especially because they are nice, nice, nices.
Mice are small, mice are fast,
And they eat our rice, rice, rices.

(Chorus)   We all love our Canadian animals, animals, animals.

We all love our beavers, beavers, beavers,
Especially because they don't have fevers, fevers, fevers.
Beavers are brown, beavers work hard,
And beavers don't ever, ever, frown.

(Chorus)   We all love our Canadian animals, animals, animals.

continued on next page

FIGURE 5–13 *continued from previous page*

The final printed copy:

Canadian Animals

One way of having children compose by formula is to have them think about writing in segments or motifs, where each segment is either a beginning, middle, or an end. When I do this activity with a group of children, I ask them to play around on their instruments, finding short chunks of four or five notes that they like, and then identifying each chunk as sounding like a beginning, middle, or end of a piece. I then ask them to notate each chunk. Sometimes I have them do this on small colored pieces of paper, with a different color for each chunk. Then I encourage them to try arranging the chunks in various patterns (e.g., blue, red, green, red, green, red, green, yellow, where blue stands for a beginning chunk, yellow for an ending, and red and green represent two different middle chunks, repeated three times each in

FIGURE 5-14 *A round*
(This round appears in *This Too Is Music*: Upitis 1990b, p. 45.)

Tiny Little Men

2, 3, or 4 part round

One day I was walking down the road and there I

saw a U. F. O. on Southwick Street.

Tiny little men came out slow___ ly

on their BIG BLUE FEET !

alternation). See Figure 5–15 for an example of a composition produced in this manner.

During this beginning-middle-end activity, some kids will try arranging the colored pieces of paper at random, and then play the resulting piece. Sometimes the results are intriguing, sometimes they are not. But in any case, it is a way of stimulating discussion about pattern and form, and even music history—I read somewhere once that Mozart used to create beginnings, middles, and ends, and then arrange them at random as a kind of a party game. If Mozart could do it . . .

I would like to describe one final example, which is not unlike

FIGURE 5–15 *A composition pieced together with beginnings, middles, and ends*
(This figure appears in *This Too Is Music*: Upitis 1990b, p. 72-73.)

The invented notation:

The piece as it would appear in standard notation:

continued on next page

FIGURE 5-15 *continued from previous page*

those described in the improvisation section earlier. An improvisation style that I use with children who have already experimented considerably with other keyboard improvisations is based on the blues scale. It is relatively simple to teach a child a **walking bass** part, and over a few days, the other notes of the scale (see Figure 5–16). If kids don't have a great deal of keyboard experience, they can take turns playing the bass and melody parts, so that two or more kids improvise at once. They can even work in the blues idiom without a keyboard, because kids have already heard enough blues music in their lives to recognize and produce the sounds with voice, especially if someone plays the accompanying walking bass on the keyboard.

Writing blues tunes works particularly well, as with most song writing, if children have an idea for a song, either from a theme that they are working on in another context, or from some other source. A case in point occurred a few years ago. I was working with a small group of children, and for some reason someone suggested rewriting the "boring nursery rhymes," titling them the *Nursery Blues*. Because the kids were already very familiar with the words of the nursery rhymes, it was easy to create new melodies. We first chanted the words in various rhythms, and then one child

FIGURE 5–16 *An activity card describing the Blues Scale*

Blues (For Two People)

HERE IS THE BASS PART FOR THE BLUES:

THE PERSON PLAYING ON THE TOP CAN PLAY ANY NOTES
INCLUDING C, E flat, F, G flat, G, or B flat:

C minor blues

sang an opening phrase. The other kids would then suggest answering phrases, and soon enough, the whole piece was generated. I had a tape recorder in the room, and it was a relatively simple matter to transcribe the melodies, add a walking bass, and produce the pieces. An example is given in Figure 5–17 (see Appendix B for the full series). I have since tried this with other groups on different themes, with similar success.

The Computer as a Writing Tool

How does the computer fit into all of this? New information technology has profoundly affected our thinking and practices in all

FIGURE 5-17 *The Nursery Blues—an excerpt*

sorts of fields, including the business of music composition. Indeed, some have argued that the computer is the most powerful tool for composition that has been developed in our history. But it is a tool that has to be considered in a broad context. If the word "computer," especially coupled with "music," makes you twinge, rest assured—it made me twinge at one time too. But I will use the rest of this chapter to explain how the computer fits as a tool with all sorts of other tools in the music composition and notation domains. For the computer is not to be ignored—now that there are at least a few computers in virtually all schools, it is of critical importance to examine how computers have been and could be used in a music environment, particularly one where composition is encouraged. Not too long ago, I wrote an article describing the use of computers in the craft of composition. Many of the points I made in that paper are addressed below. The interested reader might want to refer to the original article (Upitis 1989).

The computer is certainly not the first innovation to affect the craft of composition. Bach used to rule his manuscript paper by hand. Imagine the change when ruled staff paper became readily available many years later. Instruments that were notorious for going out of tune, such as the early violins, became much more stable as the technology of instrument making was advanced. Over the centuries, composers have used a diverse array of materials and instruments—quill, ink and paper, the voice, the lute and the drum, the guitar, the violin, and the piano. While in recent years the most significant new tools for music composition have been computer-based, these new music tools, and the digitized instruments that go along with them, do not and *should not* replace the old. It is true that new tools may do a faster job—it is much quicker to produce a score by computer than by laborious copying by hand. Sometimes new tools enable the composer to create effects with timbre that could not be produced before, forming new instruments in the process. But there are also times when the old tools, like pencil, manuscript paper, and piano (which were once new tools themselves), are best. Each has its own strengths and constraints. It is hard to imagine any single tool or instrument that could be used to perform all of the tasks associated with music composition and performance.

Which tools, computer-based or otherwise, are good tools? There are two features which I find myself considering when choosing tools for myself and for children: flexibility and an aesthetic dimension.

Good tools are flexible. By flexible, I mean that the tool should have many possible uses, both imagined and unimagined. For this reason, music software that is intended solely for the purpose of drilling elements of music theory, no matter how cleverly assembled, fails to inspire me. The opposite is true of what is often called "open-ended" or "creative" software—software which allows one to play with a motif, experiment with different arrangements for acoustic instruments, or compose a new piece of music.

Flexibility also means that one is unlikely to outgrow the tools. A woodworker will never outgrow the need for a plane. Nor do I ever expect to outgrow the need for a piano, even though I also have a synthesizer and computer, both of which I use a great deal. Computer software and computer-based instruments simply allow us to expand our collection of useful tools. While the woodworker doesn't outgrow the need for a plane, he or she may well accumulate new tools—adding a special drill or sabre saw to the collection of useful tools.

I would argue that the second feature of good tools is that they have an aesthetic quality that makes them pleasurable to use. Good tools are not merely *useful* objects, they are aesthetically *pleasing* objects. Some time ago, I watched someone screw a clamp to a pipe using a beautiful old wood handled screwdriver. I asked him to tell me about it. He told me, "It was my father's, and his father's before. A cheap plastic one does the same job, I know, but it doesn't give the same pleasure." In the same way, I far prefer my Heintzman grand piano to the old tinny 1920s bright orange upright I once owned. It is not only because the sounds are richer on the grand, although that is aesthetic reason enough. It is simply because there is more pleasure in playing an instrument that looks and feels beautiful.

So, too, should computer tools offer aesthetic appeal. For instance, I am particularly fond of the Apple Macintosh, a computer that I use for composition, graphics, and writing—the manuscript and music examples for this book were almost entirely produced on the Macintosh which sits in my upstairs study. What makes this an appealing machine? Simply put, I find that the Macintosh makes technology inviting: it asks to be touched and used. This is especially important in music, for many people, even children, do not view music as something for experimentation. Computers, on the other hand, are often regarded as "something to mess around with" and can therefore offer the opportunity to begin experimenting with sound and form in music, almost through the back door. The same is true for synthesizers. I have lost count of the number of times I have had both a synthesizer and a piano in a room, and watched those who are slightly timid of music walk straight to the synthesizer—walking by, around, or away from the piano! Because we are "allowed" to make mistakes with computers and their relatives like synthesizers, computers offer a way for people to begin engaging in those processes that enrich their musicianship, processes that may later be transferred to more traditional instruments and tools.

But I'm drifting away from the point. Back to the aesthetic qualities of computers and synthesizers as music tools. Another aesthetic feature, if you will, is that computers can be used to increase the range of sounds that can be produced by the user, especially if the computer is linked to a synthesizer or some other instrument through a MIDI (Musical Instrument Digital Interface). Sound, after all, is central to all of this, and any tool that offers opportunities to create new opportunities for playing with sound goes a long way towards enhancing the music experience. By sound, I don't mean only instrument sounds—I also mean all of those special effects sounds—ice blocks, falling stars, a dentist's drill, and the sound of knocking. Time and time again I have seen children cleverly incorporate these sounds into their compositions featuring conventional instruments and sounds, or using them as a way of illustrating dramatic improvisations.

One last aesthetic bonus. I cannot begin to describe the excitement that people exhibit when they see their compositions presented in an elegantly printed form. An excerpt from a trio for piano, clarinet, and flute, composed by an eleven-year-old, is shown in Figure 5–18 (this composition was written by the same child whose work appears earlier in the book, in Figures 2–2, 3–8, 4–10, 4–11, and 4–13). Just as children are thrilled when their books are printed, published, and, with wallpaper cover bindings, placed in the library, so too do we all thrill to seeing our compositions in print. As I mentioned earlier, all of the music examples in this book were produced in this way. There were many glowing faces when children saw their notations, along with the computer printed standard notation version, ready for publication. All of these aesthetic attributes of computer-based work—appealing tools, sounds, and products—are real and important in the craft of composition, for children and adult composers alike.

How do the issues discussed in the past few chapters regarding the development of notations and the interaction between notation and performance fit in with the computer scene? Predictably, the issues do not change, for the computer is a composition tool, and as such, is a part of the same process. If anything, the computer makes it possible for children to develop further the notations that they try to represent with pencil and paper, using simple instruments like the Orff metallophone. A few examples follow, focusing on some of the issues described earlier in this book: multiple representations, pattern and form, and the aspects relating to the composition process and the products associated therewith.

Multiple Representations

The huge variety of symbols and systems used by children (see Chapter 3) is a crucial consideration when computers become tools for children's compositions, for computers can both enhance and limit the notational forms used by children. At the moment, most software programs provide a single pre-determined notational system, often standard music notation (e.g. the *Deluxe Music Construction Set* for the Apple, Commodore, etc.). A few exceptions such as *MusicLand* (for Apple and ICON, from the Ministry of Education of Ontario), *Concertware* (for Macintosh, from Great Wave Software) and *LogoMusic* (for Apple, from Terrapin) use modified systems. *MusicLand* and the Music Player application of *Concertware* use rectangles to depict duration, where the length of the rectangle is directly proportional to the duration of the note—using the classification system described in Chapter 3, a correct and regulated but non-standard form. *LogoMusic* uses numbers and lists to show pitch and duration—another non-standard correct form. Regardless of the choice of notation, however, when using a piece of software, the child is immediately confronted with the dynamic interaction between the notation on the screen and the sounds he or she hears. Much is to be learned through this confrontation, not only by the child, but by the teacher and researcher as well. I recall, several years ago, watching children use the drumming machine on *LogoMusic* to try to "fit a beat" to familiar melodies such as *Did You Ever See a Lassie?* Because the program asked the children to use numbers both to describe the duration of the beat and the number of beats required to "cover" the whole melody, children

Underwater World
For Flute, Clarinet, and Piano — Full Score

continued on next page

FIGURE 5–18 *continued from previous page*

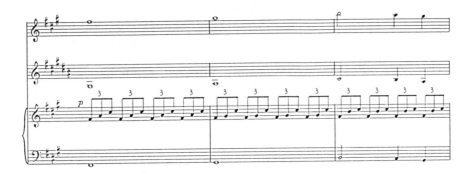

were not only making sense of beat and rhythm, but of ratios as well (Upitis 1983). It was work like this with the computer, where the notation required certain kinds of understanding, that fed into the research on children's understanding of rhythm and the notation of rhythm described in Chapter 3.

Just as researchers can learn about children's understanding of music in this way, I suspect that the more chances children have had to develop their own notations, the more they will learn from computers, where a standardized system, in one form or another, is built in. For it is through the process of relating one's own system of understanding to another's that knowledge grows, a point that has already been made many times although not in the specific context of computer tools. Ideally, a child should be given the opportunity to compare his or her notation with notations used by other children, by adults, and in computer programs as well.

Pattern and Form

A second issue which looms large in using computers as composition tools is that of the importance of pattern and form. In every composition there are patterns, and usually an overall form. Children naturally write music with pattern, employing devices such as repetition and inversion, which have been used by composers across cultures and time (see Chapters 3 and 4). When children discover the importance of pattern, either through their own writing or by comparing their compositions with others, they are often astounded by the obvious importance of their discovery. Consequently, it is very important that teachers draw attention to pattern and various devices such as repetition, **retrograde, inversion, diminution, augmentation**, and **transposition**, used to create pattern. This should be the case with and without computers. It is indisputable, however, that the use of these devices can be enhanced by using one of the many computer programs allowing such manipulations. Here the computer often does a better job than other tools. It is relatively easy for a child to take a short motif, say of four or five notes, and play it upside-down (inversion) or even backwards (retrograde) on a simple acoustic instrument. It is much more difficult to play the same motif upside-down and backwards, at least without some trial and frustration. The computer can be made to perform such a manipulation with ease, and of course, any other combination of manipulations the child may envision. I have watched children explore a motif for hours in this fashion, twisting the notes time and time again, until the original sequence is all but lost. Arguably, it is through such active self-guided exploration that children learn to control their composing, creating the effects they desire.

It is possible that the immediacy of computer notations also makes it easier for children to grasp a larger sense of form. It is difficult to hear form as one is playing the piano or an Orff instrument, as so much needs to be retained in auditory memory to do so. On the other hand, it is quite a different thing when one can see form by watching patterns emerge and relating them to one another as a graphic score is created on the screen while a piece is played. This is aptly illustrated by the following example. One seven-year-old child, in listening to the very familiar *Twinkle, Twinkle, Little Star* played on *Concertware*, noted with surprise and delight, "Oh, look at that! The first part looks the very same as the last part." No doubt, this child had heard *Twinkle, Twinkle, Little Star* many times before, but it was the new visual representation which made it possible for her to grasp the overall form of the piece. One can speculate with some assurance that such new and multiple representations of familiar material are bound to affect children's own compositions, giving structure to their exploration and use of pattern.

Further Composition Processes

In the preceding discussion, I considered some of the processes of composition that children learn through computer tools, particularly manipulating patterns and form. There are many other processes as well. Perhaps one of the most important is that of revision.

I stated earlier that teachers are now much more aware of the importance of revision in children's prose—revision in the truest sense, as opposed to mere re-copying. Computers can play an extremely useful role in sweetening the editing process to produce a handsome and well articulated final product. The same can and should occur with children's music compositions. It is not easy to revise compositions of prose or of music by hand. It is much easier to do so with computer editors. Just as children are more likely to revise their prose with a word processor, they are more likely to revise their compositions with a music editor. Even better, many music programs incorporate editing features with the others already described, so that children can not only edit, but make manipulations and see the dynamic changes in graphic notations that accompany the changing sounds.

Sometimes it is the promise of seeing their own work in a final printed form that provides the impetus for children to learn to read standard notation if they have not cared to before. This is often the case if the child has crafted a piece on a digitized instrument which the software has translated into standard notation.

There is another less obvious issue relating to process. Simply stated, it is because of the flexibility of creative computer tools that it becomes possible for the process of composition to be perceived as similar for adult and child. In some ways, working with children at the computer and having them work with me makes the process much more transparent to children than when working with traditional instruments alone. The active searching for sound and pattern, and constant revising on the computer, both serve to remove much of the mystique which, in the past, has separated composers from mere performers. When children see themselves as engaging in the same process as I, an adult composer, they come to see themselves as composers too. This is perhaps the most significant contribution that computers as tools of composition will make. I also have found that once children regard themselves as composers for computer-based instruments, they begin to see that they can compose for traditional acoustic instruments as well. I asked one ten-year-old, after he had composed many a tune on the computer, whether he would like to make up a song on the recorder. He was initially astonished at the request, saying, "You mean you can make up music on this thing?" but soon enough became absorbed in the challenge.

Moving back and forth between new and traditional instruments, and seeing oneself as a composer in relation to other composers, are both related to a third realization: Process and product are part of an infinite chain. In the past, children have tended to assume that published works are somehow finished, whether story books or printed music. However, when they enter the process of composition, they begin to see products as evolving rather than established entities. A second grade teacher recently told me that she "realized [her] kids really understood editing when [she] saw [one of her students] pencilling in a few changes to a book she had borrowed from the library."

Mixing Music and Other Symbol Systems

Many computers, including the Macintosh, which I use most often with children and for my own work, make it possible to mix music with text and pictures, both still and moving, thereby enhancing the kinds of illustrated notations that children often make even without computers (see Figure 5–19). Consider, for example, a few routes a child can take with a piece of music that he or she has played into the computer on a synthesizer connected to the computer through a MIDI interface. He or she can manipulate the notation on the screen using the mouse, or through the synthesizer, revising the music until he or she is ready to produce a final copy. But the piece of music may also be saved as a paint file, allowing the child to add illustrations and text to his or her piece through an application like *MacPaint*, in much the same way as illustrated by the notations reproduced earlier. The child may in fact combine any number of representations and ideas, linking music with graphics, text, and movement. The music can be performed by the computer or on other instruments, and the computer can be made to perform conditionally and predictably in a way that live performers, at least those at the disposal of most children, may not.

The variety of sounds that can be generated by the computer and synthesizer are also varied and tantalizing. I have seen many

FIGURE 5–19 *A composition with an illustration*

an idea born simply as a result of a child's messing about with preset timbres or by manipulating sound parameters through the software. The breadth of possibilities presented by a computer system helps deliver the message that music is more than just notes on a page or a piece performed on piano or by computer, but is even richer when integrated with drawings and stories, movement and drama. The computer, used in this fashion, can do much to erode the boundaries of school subject domains, of acoustic versus digital instruments, of composers versus performers, of music consumers versus music makers. At the same time, the power of computer processing, memory, and ease and immediacy of feedback, make it possible to explore deeply the complexities of music itself.

Concluding Remarks

In designing activities to enhance notation and composition, and in the search for powerful tools of music technology to aid in those activities, it is critical that we not lose sight of the craft itself. The creative part of us should come through whether on laser printouts or notes scratched out by hand, whether in writing trios for acoustic instruments, soundscapes for voice and rhythm band instruments, or writing the *Nursery Blues*. If the computer has a role to play in the crafts of children, it is to make the creation and sharing of their works more accessible. Most important, children's compositions, both produced on computers and on traditional instruments, must be a part of a larger music experience, with the primary emphasis not on computers, nor perhaps even on composition and notation, but on making music.

A Whole Music
Approach to
Becoming a Musician

▲▲▲▲▲▲▲▲▲▲▲▲▲▲▲▲▲▲ In the previous chapter, I described the written aspects of what might be seen as a "whole music" approach, paralleling that of whole language. I can think of several related reasons for adopting this approach to music, especially at this point in the developing history of music education, and indeed, of our culture.

To begin with, there is such a deservedly strong movement to teaching written expression through children's own writing, that it only makes sense to see how such a view can be incorporated into another discipline where writing is—or should be—important. Not only is there promise in a whole language approach in developing children's abilities to compose, but in fact, by taking such an approach, the whole enterprise of composition thereby becomes something worthy of notice. It would now be a foreign thought for many of us to imagine teaching writing without having children actively engage in writing. Many fine books and articles have been written with this approach in mind, relating teaching practices, examples of children's writing, and various ways of dealing with problems of the process of writing and the evaluation of the same (e.g., Altwerger, Edelsky, & Flores 1987; Atwell 1987; Calkins 1983, 1986; Goodman 1986; Graves 1983; Mills & Clyde 1990; Murray 1985; Newman 1983; Newman & Church 1990). With the current strength of this view, the time has come to consider how the teaching of music might be substantially altered should the importance of composition be similarly acknowledged. I argued in the past chapter that using computers as part of the process might open doors (even back doors) to creating music. That is, while some children and adults might be hesitant to improvise and compose on traditional instruments, this hesitancy is often lessened when the instruments are ones where experimentation is expected. In a similar way, if teachers are accustomed to successfully having children create original works in language, they might be convinced by the successes they witness in a language context, to apply the same approach to music. And perhaps most important of all, using this kind of approach to the teaching and learning of music simply makes sense. Because we want children to use language, we expect them to be readers, writers, critics, and creators. If we want children to be musicians, using music as a means of making and conveying meaning, then they should be musicians from the start—improvisers, composers, notators, performers, listeners, critics, and music creators in the broadest way.

The teaching approaches and ideas, research, examples, and stories in this book have been primarily focused on aspects of music notation. Issues of performance and improvisation have, of course, been discussed since they are inseparable from the process of developing notations. But in the same way that a whole language and process writing approach includes all of the related aspects of writing—reading, editing, revising, sharing, and being surrounded by literature, there is a parallel need for music experiences beyond notation and composition. Simply put, no matter how fascinating the process of notational development becomes, one cannot get so wrapped up in issues of notation that the music-making is forgotten. Not everything needs to be recorded. Not everything needs to be notated. Not everything needs to be remembered. Not everything needs to be shared.

I have talked about other kinds of activities that support composition and notation both in the present context and in another book (Upitis 1990b). These include all of those enterprises like sharing through impromptu and formal performance, singing, instrument making, listening, incorporating music with movement and drama, relating music to poetry and mathematics, using music for storytelling, and so on, all of which contribute to a lively and generative music community. Rather than repeating descriptions of these ventures, I will instead look briefly at two of the intertwining roles musicians play, roles besides those of composer and notator, which I have already discussed at length. But even though the next few stories are of children as improvisers and critics, these are roles that would have been less likely, at least for the children described, had they not been composers and notators as well.

About eight months ago, I began teaching a nine-year-old boy named David. His was, in Holt's words, "asked-for learning"—for a year he had been asking his parents if he could learn to play the piano. An earlier episode with violin lessons had not gone well, and his parents had some hesitations. But they convinced themselves that it was worth a try, thinking that David was older and that I might be the kind of piano teacher that David would like. And so, we began our lessons. At the beginning, David was very quiet, and like many kids, not at all comfortable with *playing* the piano. At his first lesson, he sat up straight on the bench, hands on his lap, waiting for me to tell him what to play. When I launched into my usual opening—"Let's try some improvisation"—he was more hesitant than most. Getting him to play around with any of the notes, even the foolproof pentatonic scale (see Chapter 5), was difficult. But in a few weeks' time, the power of having control over the instrument took hold, and David was well on the way to becoming an improviser, composer, and performer. After a couple of months, his mother told me that he "never walks by the piano without playing a few notes." At lessons, getting him to stop long enough to listen to what I had to say had become the norm. At this time, he also began to talk a good deal about what it was like to take piano lessons. He asked me many questions, all in the vein of "Can you get other people to teach like this?" and commented thereafter, "Most teachers don't teach like this. Like, not how to play, but the notes and stuff . . . not learning the first day or anything." David had it all figured out—or almost all of it. Yes, I was teaching him to play. But he was also learning the "notes and stuff" from the playing. And making music was becoming a more central part of his life. David's lessons are on Tuesdays, and that year, Christmas Day fell on a Tuesday. "Oh wow," said he, "Christmas is on my music day!" (followed by some surprise when I told him I wouldn't be coming for that lesson).

Another related role that children come to take is that of critic. Again, I am convinced that this arises in large measure from being taken seriously as music makers—improvisers, composers, performers. One of the children I have taught for many years (the same one who made the music scribbles in Figure 2–2, and later wrote the trio for clarinet, flute, and piano in Figure 5–18) recently took a conservatory exam in piano. At the same time, I was taking a voice exam myself, so a special bond existed between us by being in the same boat. Although I was teacher to her, I was clearly also a fellow learner. As a part of all of this we regularly listened to each other, commenting on one another's performances. When our exams were looming, this process was stepped up a bit, with extra lessons and so on. At one point, Beatrice taped herself playing her repertoire, as she had seen me do for my singing, and proceeded to write comments about her performance. It was a magnificent reminder to me that we can be our own best critics, and a further reminder that children are just as capable of criticizing their own work as adults are of theirs. Her comments were, in her own terms, often of the same essence as those made by her examiner a week or so later. But Bea's comments also reflected her view of music as negotiable and evolving—she knew well when she was doing something that was not the composer's intention, but nevertheless, made a choice she felt convinced enough to take. These kinds of choices, I am sure, would not be made as comfortably by a child who was not herself a composer. Some of her comments, and those of the examiner, appear below:

Sarabande

BEATRICE: More melodie in right hand. End trill more trilly.
EXAMINER: The right hand melody must sing out more...
Some stylish playing.

Sonatina

BEATRICE: Remember chords at the end of the runs. Get runs smoother. Good dynamics! Don't run away with right hand!
EXAMINER: Work on scale passages...good dynamic contrasts.

Study No. 5

BEATRICE: More dynamics. Not too fast. Don't plunk trills.
EXAMINER: Aim for some variety in dynamic level...

Study No. 6

BEATRICE: Not too much pedal. Good ending. Not too fast!!!!
  Good dynamics but they're mostly invented.
EXAMINER: Good pedalling . . .

Beatrice, of course, is not alone in making choices as a performer. While one expects that performers would make decisions regarding such things as dynamics, when children are composers, they take even further liberties in their performances of the works of others. Joel, in learning a simple piece called *The Rider*, commented, "Well, I don't play it exactly how the notes say, but it sounds good anyway." Hilary, at the age of six, in similar circumstances commented, "I put in a few changes. Instead of one note in this hand I'm putting two." Finally, I have often told the story of the child who edited the end of a Beethoven Sonatina because "[it] could have been a better ending." It is not that these children are in some way disrespectful of the works of others. Rather, because they are composers themselves, they critically examine the compositions of others with their own eyes, making changes and always acknowledging "their way" and "my way" in the process of taking someone else's work as seriously as their own. And in so doing, they are constructing knowledge, making meaning, inventing ways of understanding—all of those powerful means of living and learning that have been considered in the earlier chapters of this book. This was described to me once by an adult student, learning how to play the piano through improvisation and composition (hers is the second piece which appears in Figure 5–9) in the following way;

> It's not just that I'm learning about the subject—piano or music—I'm learning about myself. How I process information, what situations make me anxious or nervous, and when I've had enough and I just need to tune out. I always have to be able to fit whatever I learn into the whole scheme of things. What are the connections? How does this fit with all the other things I know? I need to see patterns. And that's what I'm learning.

A final comment. When I am reading a book that is printed and published, and enjoying it, it often seems to me that the writing is somehow effortless. What is said is written in such a way that it seems as if it could read no other way, and indeed, that the words must have just flowed in an uninterrupted stream from the author's mind. But writing books is not like that. Nor is writing music. Nor is playing music—but what a skill it is to make it sound so. As a teenager, I was once struggling to learn a Haydn Sonata. After proudly pulling off the first movement, I turned to my piano teacher for approval and praise. Mrs. Ferguson, my piano teacher, said, "Good. Now make it sound easy." I blurted out that it wasn't easy. And her response? "Of course not, dear, but you have to make it sound that way." Once in a while, it is true, a segment will flow, whether in writing, composing, playing music, painting, or whatever, and as such, need little reworking. But we frequently underestimate how hard the process can be, especially when the final product seems so effortless.

The difficulty does not mean that writing is without re-wards—I like to write, even though it is sometimes hard. But it is not just the process of the writing that is of concern. There were times when I was writing the earlier chapters of this book that I doubted the very *purpose* for writing a book such as this, never mind the difficulties one encounters in the process. I found myself continually asking why this work has been so important to me for so long, and if in fact it would be important to others. At times, I found it hard to find the significance of the work, and therefore the words to relate that significance. This was especially true at a time when the bombs began raining in the Middle East, a time when writing a book about notation seemed, on some level, sense-less. But it is not. Even when we are disturbed by global events, it is still important to undertake what we do in our daily lives with passion and commitment. Like the cycles and oscillations of learn-ing, where we move from integration to specialization, from play to reflection, from the broad to the narrow, or here, from the local to the global, our research and teaching also works within these cycles and tensions.

This work is important because music is important. Music is a part of *everyone*'s life. In different ways, all of us like music. And use music. Even though I have enjoyed writing this book, and indeed, have coveted the hours when I have been able to sit down long enough to write a few pages, that time is always punctuated by breaks—breaks that include taking long walks, cooking a pot of soup on the woodstove, and making music. Music is a part of me. I cannot imagine a day without music. Even on the days that I don't sing, or play the 'cello or piano, I listen to music, or write some. I need music when I am sad, when I am happy, when I am quiet, when I am filled with energy. Music is a way of interpreting our world, a way of expanding our understanding of the world, our stories, our relationships, our knowledge, our values. It is a way of making sense in a potential space, a kind of knowing, a voice. It is even a way to think about the Middle East. It is this sense of music that I hope to pass on to my students, as my teachers have done for me.

And notation? If notation is important at all in this process, it is important as an integral part of the craft of making music. When a child comes up to me, notation and instrument in hand, and says, "Can I play you my song?" the question signifies much more than a request for a minute or two of my attention. It means, "Listen to what I made up, look at how I wrote it down, see what I can do, and—most important of all—listen to who I am."

▲ ▲

Appendix A:
Issues of General
Cognitive Growth

▲ ▲ ▲ ▲ ▲ ▲ ▲ ▲ ▲ ▲ ▲ ▲ ▲ ▲ ▲ ▲ ▲ ▲ MANY thinkers have written re-markable books on children's development, and I cannot hope to do justice to them all in this context, nor will I try. I do intend, however, to give a sense of the kinds of issues that relate to and inspire my work on composition and notation, and to refer the interested reader to other sources.

What strikes me most about the works I am about to describe, and the issues raised by the writers cited, is that each time I read or re-read one of these treatises, I am newly reminded of how much children can do—how much they think about, how inventive are their ways of walking through the world, and in terms of the focus of this book, how well they represent what they think through the use of symbols. Spending time with children when they are free to explore and create has the same effect—I still marvel, as do others, at what we have to learn from watching children at work, at *their* work (see Wallace 1990).

When I was recently reaquainting myself with the works of
Piaget (1941, 1952, 1955, 1962), Donaldson (1980), Hawkins (1974),
Whitehead (1929), Armstrong (1981), Dewey (1902), Vygotsky
(1934), Wells (1986), Papert (1980), Holt (1967, 1976), and Falbel
(1989), and reading for the first time books by Bruner (1990), Connelly and Clandinin (1988), Newman, Griffin, and Cole (1989),
Hodgkin (1985), and others, I was reading with an eye for common
themes in terms of features of cognitive development that would
apply specifically to the development of music notation. While
there were many such possibilities, I have elected to describe only
a few here.

One notion that emerges again and again, is that when children and adults are actively pursuing their own enterprises, they
are inventors and explorers in the fullest sense. Hodgkin (1985)
observes;

> The world will almost certainly be physically hard for most of
> our children and grandchildren; it will be intellectually and spir-
> itually hard for all of them. This has always been so—more or
> less—but it has been especially so at times of profound change.
> So resilience (which can be defined as adaptability combined with
> integrity)—physical, intellectual and spiritual resilience—should
> be an underlying aim of all education. This is why the myth of
> Robinson Crusoe . . . is so apt . . . Think, if you can, of these three
> images in the same breath: Robinson Crusoe making sense of his
> island, a teenager exploring his or her chosen wilderness and a
> one year old infant being helped to make sense of some intriguing
> new play space. The desire of each to survive, to grow and to
> find more truth, is part of their very essence as they interact with
> that bit of the universe which faces them. And it is first and
> foremost a peopled universe. The isolation of these desert islands
> is a conceit, reminding us that humans are not, in essence, victims
> but responsible *agents* within a society, within a culture; and this
> means that they are, above all, co-operative doers and makers,
> and lovers.(16–17)

Kinds of Knowing

Within this framework of inventiveness and exploration, educators, philosophers, and psychologists have identified different
kinds of knowledge or knowing. Piaget, for example, outlined what
he saw as stages of intellectual development as they applied to
various domains—such as number, space, time, distance, play,
dreams, movement, and speed. In observing his own children over

a period of many years, he noted that they moved from what he termed *sensori-motor* knowledge to *operational* knowledge of several forms, and finally, to a stage he called *formal operations* (Piaget 1947). At each of these stages of intelligence or knowing, Piaget observed that children were convinced that their beliefs were right, and tenaciously argued when challenged. For instance, in the classic water conservation task, Piaget placed three cylinders in front of the child, two short wide ones and one tall thin one. The two short cylinders were filled with equal amounts of water. The tall cylinder was empty. When Piaget poured water from one of the short cylinders to the tall one, children who had not reached what he termed the "conservation" stage, claimed that there was now *more* water in the tall cylinder than in the other short cylinder, *even though they had watched him pour the water from one cylinder to the other.* This finding surprised, and still surprises, many people. But what is perhaps even more important than the "incorrectness" of the child's knowledge, is that the belief of the child, at this stage, is so unshakable. At this stage, one could even argue that the child's knowledge was "right," given what he or she had experienced and theorized from those experiences. This kind of knowing is also relevant to notations, for some children who represent rhythms figurally will argue that metric representations are wrong—not unlike arguing that there is more water in the tall cylinder. In terms of understanding rhythm notations, I would argue further that it is critically important that the children be allowed and encouraged to explore their beliefs in the system they have embraced, so that later, they can use that knowledge to develop new ways of knowing.

Although many have disputed the specifics of Piaget's theories of intelligence since they were first developed (e.g., Donaldson 1980), educators and psychologists nevertheless remain indebted to him, for Piaget successfully challenged the earlier simplistic and mechanistic views of learning and intelligence, and instead, turned his attention towards careful and caring observation of individual children, honoring their knowing by examining closely their systems of beliefs. Since Piaget's extensive work with children, numerous other views of knowing have emerged. Most of these views describe a kind of knowledge that, like the work of Piaget, draw attention to the specific context of the learner, not only in terms of the experiences he or she has had, but also in terms of the social structures within which the learning has taken place, and knowledge which is articulated versus knowledge which is tacit. Polanyi (1958), for example, is well known for his writing on *tacit knowledge*, that is, the underlying mass of experience, attitudes, and skills, physical and intellectual, that develop uniquely in each person through the process of engaging in skilled acts of making, discovering, and judging. Polanyi gives many examples of tacit knowledge, such as being able to use a hammer, or driving a car—both are skills that become automatic or tacit, although at the beginning, were difficult. Similarly, Schön (1983) speaks of the knowledge of practice in *The Reflective Practitioner*. Recently, Connelly and Clandinin (1988) have described a similar kind of knowing specifically in terms of the teaching profession. Once again, they describe this kind of knowing as something that is evidenced in practice, but may be difficult to articulate. They use the term *personal practical knowledge* to talk about the knowledge of teachers, again highlighting the importance of the role of experience.

Another approach in describing the complexity of intelligence or knowing has been taken by those who have delineated multiple kinds of intelligences. One of the most well known recent theories of this type is that of Gardner (1983). In his book *Frames of Mind: A Theory of Multiple Intelligences*, Gardner describes what he sees as seven qualitatively different kinds of knowing: linguistic, logical-mathematical, musical, spatial, bodily-kinaesthetic, intrapersonal, and interpersonal. Others have outlined similar types of human competencies. For example, Hodgkin (1985) refers to five areas: language-like, musical, iconic, enactive, and interpersonal knowing and representation. But what is important here is not to come to agreement about the kinds of knowing *per se*, but to examine what features these views share in common. First, there is acknowledgment of the importance of language, and that language and thought are inseparable (see also Vygotsky 1934, in this regard). Second, there are some domains that are seen as qualitatively different from others, e.g., logical-mathematical and musical. Finally, there is a clear acknowledgment, in attempting to describe ways of knowing, of the importance of both inter- and intrapersonal interaction, and culture. For this reason, other ways of knowing and voices to express that knowing, such as those advanced by feminist thinkers (e.g., Belenky, Clinchy, Goldberger, & Tarule 1986; Gilligan 1982) fit into this general scheme of knowledge. That is, various forms of intelligence or knowing become important when the whole enterprise of human thought and interaction is considered. Further, these ways of knowing, while distinct in nature, are not isolated from each other, but linked through the bond of human experience.

Ways of Learning

Given that ways of knowing are complex, and embedded in social experience, how, then, do we learn? And learn new ways of knowing? Here two prevailing notions appear throughout the literature. The first is that in building knowledge, humans make extensive use of tools and symbols. The second is that learning is most likely to occur at particular times and in specific contexts and circumstances.

Those educators who believe that children learn science and mathematics by manipulating objects are supported by the theorists who speak of the importance of toys, tools, and symbols. One of the best descriptions I have come across for integrating toy, tool, symbols, and play, practice, and meaning is given by Hodgkin (1985). Hodgkin claims that for infants, toy, tool, and symbol are undifferentiated. He argues that it is only through play and creation that toys become either symbols or tools. He does not (nor do I) see toy-tool-symbol as a linear progression, but rather, that through play, toys take on a different kind of meaning. If the play is exploratory, Hodgkin claims that the toys can become symbols. That is, through exploration, these new experiences can be accommodated through symbolic development. On the other hand, if the play leads to practice, then the outcome is different: the toy becomes a tool, and competencies are developed and solidified. Thus, a musical instrument, which begins as a toy, can become a tool for performance if one practices certain skills enough, or it can become a way of exploring music through improvisation and composition, and the symbols generated in the process of those pursuits. In Hodgkin's terms (and those of others, such as Langer [1957] and Jung [1946]), symbols not only carry meaning, but are lively extensions of our personal being. He writes:

> [A symbol is] not only something which we grasp and use and make an extension of ourselves, it is also at the same time part of what we are exploring or creating. It has two faces. It is 'me' and 'not me'—part of the changing universe which I, through it, am disturbing. In this tradition, therefore, the symbol should not be thought of as merely a sign, which is what Piaget does when he defines a symbol as having some resemblance to objects or events. . . . Symbols do often have resemblance to what is signified but the profounder, more dynamic meaning of the word is properly stressed by analytical psychologists. Jung is emphatic that symbols are, metaphorically speaking, 'alive'; they have a

transforming, retroactive effect on their users. . . . A great deal depends on the context . . . in which they are being used. (Hodgkin 1985, 54–55)

And in what kind of context can symbols come alive in the way that Hodgkin and Jung describe? I now turn to a discussion of context—the second common notion discussed by those interested in the construction of intelligence.

Again, there is a profusion of terms describing essentially the same phenomenon, namely, that we learn in a "field" that is defined by space, time, and culture. Polanyi (1958) referred to this as a *heuristic field*, a place where discoveries can be made. Vygotksy (1934) described a *zone of proximal development*, where two or more people, linked by a shared activity, discover something new. Hodgkin (1985) speaks of *potential space*, where the learner, by moving towards a dimly perceived frontier, through play, practice, and exploration, develops skills and competence—"room to be and to become" (p. 24). Newman, Griffin, and Cole (1989) speak of the *construction zone*, "a magic place where minds meet, where things are not the same to all who see them, where meanings are fluid, and where one person's construal may preempt another's" (White, in Newman, Griffin & Cole 1989, ix).

All of the above descriptions are again more similar than different, and they lead to similar outcomes in terms of the kinds of opportunities that educators should provide. Teachers, parents, or others with specialized crafts or knowledge belong in the potential space as people for children to interact with, and as people who are subject to feedback from the learners. Hodgkin (1985) claims that the teacher is "responsible both for making and protecting the child's space and for introducing into it appropriate structural elements which derive from the surrounding culture" (p. 26). In terms of music education specifically, Davidson and Scripp (1988b) propose a view that is congruent with this notion of potential space. After analyzing several current music pedagogy practices, from a cognitive-developmental point of view, they offer several criteria for evaluating pedagogical alternatives. These include the possibility of multiple representations of musical knowledge, opportunities for performance, instruction, composition, representation, and reflective thought. Generally, they state that "we need a model for music education that effectively energizes the child in all manifestations of our musical culture" (Davidson & Scripp 1988b, 84).

I have chosen to end this section with yet another quotation from Hodgkin's (1985) work (I really like his ideas!), linking together the notions of potential space and the frontiers of learning, the social nature of learning, and returning once again to his Robinson Crusoe metaphor. Hodgkin writes:

[I would like to emphasize] the frontier of exploration which limits a learner's field of knowledge. The reason for this 'focus on frontiers' (Goodman, 1969, p. 259) is that teachers need to develop a special sensitivity to the reality and importance of the 'high tide' aspect of every learner, even though it only appears twice a month. One difficulty about the frontier emphasis and the whole desert island picture is that it can deflect our attention away from the essentially social and cultural nature of education. . . . The Crusoe metaphor reminds us, in the first place, that someone who survives a shipwreck, who is 'forced' to explore new ground, is not to be seen as a victim, as being moulded, nor is he a superman, moulding everything. He or she is a complex, self-motivated individual, interacting with an extremely problematic world. Too many discussions of education omit this and swing away from the interactive middle ground towards those false antitheses of victim versus exploiter. . . . The Crusoe metaphor is also useful in helping us to think about the ways in which chance and orderliness interact. (Hodgkin 1985, 14–15).

Cycles of Understanding

In developing knowledge within a "heuristic field" or "potential space," there is another feature of learning which bears discussion. Many writers have identified cycles of understanding. Whitehead (1929) speaks of knowledge beginning with the stage of romance, where the learner is intrigued by the novelty of the subject or inquiry, and where explorations are not dominated by systematic procedures but by the immediacy of the materials and questions at hand. This is followed by a time of precision, where, in his words, the "width of relationship is subordinated to exactness of formulation" (Whitehead 1929, 18). Finally, Whitehead sees a need for generalization, applying those concepts and principles honed during the stage of precision to other areas, reaching a synthesis of some form. And then, he argues, the cycle begins again, as the learner returns to romanticism with the "added advantage of classified ideas and relevant technique" (Whitehead 1929, 19). This is not unlike the three cyclical phases described by Hawkins, a science educator, nearly fifty years later. Again, the need for free and unguided exploration, or just plain "messing about" is emphasized (Hawkins 1974, 67). This messing about phase leads to a time which is

> ...more externally guided and disciplined [by] multiple programmed material ... that contains written and pictorial guidance of some sort, but which is designed ... so that for almost any given way into a subject that a child may evolve on his own, there is material available which he will recognize as helping him farther along that very way. (Hawkins 1974, 71)

Finally, Hawkins argues for time for discussion and theorizing, which, of course, may well lead back to "messing about." Other educators and researchers, while not necessarily identifying three intermingling and cyclical stages, nevertheless describe the tension between these different kinds of investigation. Hodgkin (1985) speaks of the "irregular oscillation between extreme boldness and times of cautious reflection" (p. 9). Davidson and Scripp (1988b) state that "change occurs in alternating phases of stability and instability" (p. 62). This tension or oscillation has been observed specifically in the area of music as well. Swanwick and Tillman (1986) claim that in improvisation, children move from a self-absorbed exploration of materials to reflection on materials used to solve problems of music expression.

In terms of teaching and learning environments, I take these observations about cycles and oscillations to mean that the learning environment should provide opportunities for both *exposure* to new artifacts and ideas, and opportunities for *intervention* on the part of the teacher and others. Too often in traditional teaching, we have been concerned with interventions, and haven't allowed enough time for the exposure that comes through play. Equally troublesome is the emphasis on play and integration without any time for specialization, deep thought and criticism—which, of course, can and probably should still be playful and explorative in nature. Or, as Hodgkin (1985) states, "enjoyable practice does not have to be lacking in rigour" (p. 45) "[and] ... play is there at the beginning, and it remains central" (p. 52). Teachers who promote the integration of subjects, in contrast to those who state that there must be specialization for learning to occur, are both "right"—both kinds of learning opportunities are important. In Whitehead's terms, integration occurs in two ways, in the romantic stage when a discipline or an idea is new, and again at the stage of generalization, which in turn can lead to a new romanticism, beginning the cycle again. But there is specialization as well, in the part of the cycle that he calls the stage of precision—the time of external multiple programming in Hawkins's terms.

In closing, I'd like to point to an even broader picture of learning and research that is becoming increasingly prevalent as we approach the end of the twentieth century, one that I find not only attractive but essentially important to adopt if we are to honor children as learners within a culture. Just as Hodgkin (1985) observed that we are responsible agents within a society and culture, Bruner (1990) is newly concerned with issues of culture in terms of cognitive development. Bruner (1990) cautions with great eloquence the dangers in continuing with our present directions in cognitive psychology, where research has become a series of "intellectually unsituated little studies . . . [and where] the achievement of a causal explanation forces us to artificialize what we are studying to a point almost beyond recognition as representative of human life" (p. xi–xiii). He notes that the "great psychological questions are being raised once again—questions about the nature of mind and its processes, questions about how we construct our meanings and our realities, questions about the shaping of mind by history and culture . . . [and that we] must venture beyond the conventional aims of positivist science with its ideals of reductionism . . . [and move towards] a study of all and every aspect of the meaning-making process . . . a cultural psychology" (Bruner, 1990, xi–xiii).

One of the current movements, rapidly gaining strength, that counteracts this narrow and reductionistic view of research and learning is that of narrative inquiry (see Bateson 1989; Connelly & Clandinin 1988; and Polkinghorne 1988, to name but a few). Here it is argued by anthropologists, psychologists, therapists, linguists, medical and legal practitioners, sociologists, historians, and educators alike, that people are essentially storytellers. If we ignore their stories, we not only do them an injustice, but we fail to take advantage of an opportunity to make meaning and effect change. Further, people have argued that through narrative, some of the distance that has grown between theory and practice can be bridged. Polkinghorne writes

> I view my discipline, psychology, as a unified enterprise, and have supported the ideal of the integration of its scientific and professional aspects; yet I have not found the findings of academic research of much help in my work as a clinician . . . My own un-

settled feelings about integrating research and practice are not idiosyncratic... Academics and practitioners seem to be growing increasingly separate, and my discipline's organization... has begun to institutionalize their division... Despite the general lessening of confidence in the ability of social science research to provide useful answers to human problems, people increasingly have been turning for help to the practitioners... [who]... are better commonsense epistemologists than academics. What I found was that practitioners work with narrative knowledge.... Narrative [is] the primary form by which human experience is made meaningful. (1988, ix–x; 1)

In this book, I have attempted to begin bridging the mass of research literature on children's notation with the equally large mass of stories from the practice of teaching music notation. For like Polkinghorne and many others, I believe that through story we can unravel the tangles in a given area of interest, and in so doing, weave a new understanding that is more highly textured and ultimately more interesting.

▲▲▲▲▲▲▲▲▲▲▲▲▲▲▲▲▲▲▲▲▲▲▲▲▲

Appendix B:
The Nursery Blues

Music: *Rena Upitis*
     Jennifer Clark
     Alice Oliver
     Rebecca Oliver
     Nathan Taylor
     Bobbie West

Cartoons: *Bruce Patterson*

Calligraphy: *Catherine Barney*

Mary Had a Little Lamb

♩=144

Ma-ry had a lit-tle lamb whose fleece was white as snow And every—where that Mary went the lamb was sure — to go —

1.

to go —

2.

2. He followed her to school one day,
   (which was against the rules).
   And all the children laughed and played,
   To see a lamb at school!

♩ = 150　*Three (Six, Nine, Twelve...) Blind Mice*

Sing a Song of Sixpence

♩. = 75

Sing a song of six-pence a
poc— ket full of rye   Four and twen- ty blackbirds
Baked into a pie ——— And when the pie was opened ——— the
birds be-gan to sing ——— what a dainty di—sh to

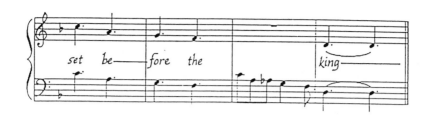

set be—fore the   king——

Jill   came   tum ———————

———————— bling   after !

▲ ▲

Glossary of Musical Terms

Accidental

The signs used in standard notation ($\sharp$, $\flat$, $\natural$) to either raise a note or lower a note by a semi-tone. If an accidental applies all the way through the composition, it appears at the beginning in the key signature. Otherwise, accidentals that apply for only a note or two appear next to the note(s) in the composition. (See *flat, sharp*.)

Alto Clef

A marking at the beginning of a line of music indicating the relative pitches of each note on the staff. The alto clef, also known as a C clef, has two brackets which surround the line for the note C. The notes falling within the alto clef are medium high, corresponding to alto vocal music, viola string music, and so on. (See also *tenor clef, bass clef,* and *treble clef*.)

Augmentation

This refers to the operation of changing all of the durations of a piece of music so that they are all proportionally longer. That is, if a note was originally a quarter note, and the piece was augmented by doubling the durations, the quarter note would become a half note. This has the effect of making the composition sound slower than the original.

Bass Clef
A marking at the beginning of a line of music indicating the relative pitches of each note on the staff. The bass clef, also known as the F clef, has two dots around the line for the note F. The notes falling within the bass clef are low, corresponding to bass vocal music, double bass string music, and so on. (See also *treble clef, alto clef, and tenor clef.*)

Broken Form
When all of the notes of a chord are played separately (e.g., C, E, G) the chord is said to be in broken form. (See *solid form.*)

Diminution
This refers to the operation of changing all of the durations of a piece of music so that they are all proportionally shorter. That is, if a note was originally a quarter note, and diminution was performed by halving the durations, the quarter note would become an eighth note. This has the effect of making the composition sound faster than the original.

Chord
Two or more notes played at once or in sequence. (See *broken form* and *solid form.*)

Double Barline
Two vertical lines at the end of a piece of music indicating the end of the piece.

Duration
The length of a note or rest. Durations can be thought of in terms of the time signature of the piece. Thus in 3/4 time, there are three quarter notes in a bar, each receiving one beat. A half note is twice as long as a quarter note (in 3/4 time, a half note would take up two-thirds of the bar; while in 4/4 time or common time, it would take up half the bar). Other common durations are eighth notes, dotted half notes, whole notes, and sixteenth notes. There are rests

corresponding to each type of note (see Figure 5–4). (See *pitch, time signature*.)

Dynamics
A general term referring to loudness-softness. Dynamics refers to both a general volume level (e.g., *mezzo forte* means medium loud in Italian—most music terms come from Italian), and to gradual and sudden changes in volume (e.g., *diminuendo* means gradually getting softer; *p subito* means suddenly softly).

Figural Notation
Refers to a form of rhythm notation where the events are grouped according to how they sound in relation to each other, forming chunks or figures, rather than being represented in terms of relative durations (see Chapter 3 for a lengthy explanation of this idea; also Figure 3–1).

Flat
A sign (♭) placed before a note, indicating that the note to be sung or played is a semi-tone lower than the note. On the keyboard, this kind of accidental most often applies to the black keys. In English, this means that an A♭ is the black key immediately to the left, i.e., below, the white note A.

Glissando
Playing a scale quickly with a sliding movement. On the xylophone or metallophone, this means running the mallot across the keys (either up or down). On the piano, a glissando is usually played by drawing the thumb nail or the nail of the middle finger across either the black or the white keys. Glissandi are also commonly played by harpists.

Harmony
A collection of pitches played together. Usually one thinks of harmony as pleasant sounding chords, but harmony more generally refers to the vertical dimension of music, i.e., the notes that sound together in supporting or embellishing a melody.

Interval
The distance between two pitches. For example, the note C to F is an interval of a perfect fourth. Intervals can be major, minor, per-

fect, augmented, or diminished. The most commonly referred to intervals fall within an octave, i.e., the first, second, third, fourth, fifth, sixth, seventh, and eighth or octave. Naming intervals is a tricky business, and for the purposes of this glossary, a bit too complicated an explanation to tackle.

Inversion
Taking a melody or a chunk of a melody and playing it upside-down.

Major
Refers to a collection of notes forming a key. When a piece is written in a major key, the notes are all mixed up in the melody, but it usually ends on the tonic, the note from which key takes its name. When all of the notes in a major key are played sequentially, the result is a major scale. It can be described by a pattern of tones and semi-tones (T, T, S, T, T, T, S), and is the same going up as it is coming down (i.e., the T, S, combinations in the example, in the reverse order). A good deal of Western music is written in major keys, and there are lots of examples in this book (e.g., see Figures 1–6, 1–8, 1–9 for common children's melodies in the key of C major).

Melody
A collection of pitches played in sequence (as opposed to harmony, which refers to pitches played simultaneously). Colloquially, people also refer to melody as the "tune."

Metric Notation
Refers to a form of rhythm notation where the events are depicted according to their measured durations relative to an underlying beat (see Chapter 3 for a lengthy explanation of this idea; also Figure 3–1). Standard music notation is of a metric form. (See *time signature*.)

Minor, harmonic
Refers to a collection of notes forming a certain type of minor key. When a piece is written in a harmonic minor key, the notes are all mixed up in the melody, but it usually ends on the tonic, the note from which key takes its name. Compositions that are written in harmonic minor keys, and indeed, melodic minors as well, are

distinguishable from major keys by the accidentals that are usually scattered throughout the piece. These accidentals usually serve the function of raising the seventh note a semi-tone, giving the harmonic minor its identifiable character.

When all of the notes in a harmonic key are played sequentially, the result is a harmonic minor scale. It can be described by a pattern of tones and semi-tones (T, S, T, T, S, T+S, S), and is the same going up as it is coming down (i.e., the T, S, combinations in the example, in the reverse order). Kids often describe pieces written in a minor key as sad.

Minor, melodic
Refers to a collection of notes forming a certain type of minor key. When a piece is written in a melodic minor key, the notes are all mixed up in the melody, but it usually ends on the tonic, the note from which the key takes its name. When all of the notes in a melodic minor key are played sequentially, the result is a melodic minor scale. It can be described by a pattern of tones and semi-tones; going up (T, S, T, T, T, T, S), and coming down (T, T, S, T, T, S, T). Coming down, the notes are the same in the melodic minor as in the relative major, that is, the major key that shares the same key signature (complicated enough?).

Minor, natural
Refers to a collection of notes forming a certain type of minor key. When a piece is written in a natural minor key, the notes are all mixed up in the melody, but it usually ends on the tonic, the note from which the key takes its name. When all of the notes of a natural minor key are played sequentially, the result is a natural minor scale. It can be described by a pattern of tones and semi-tones (T, S, T, T, S, T, T), and is the same going up as it is coming down (i.e., the T, S, combination in the example, in the reverse order). Unlike the harmonic minor and the melodic minor going up, the seventh note in the natural minor is not raised by an extra accidental. That is, the only notes in the natural minor are those that appear in the key signature.

Minuet
A French country dance, which became very popular in Europe in the seventeenth century. Minuets are in 3/4 time, and while they were originally played in a moderate tempo, Mozart and Haydn used a faster form of the Minuet in their symphonies.

Octave

The interval from a note to the next note of the same name. An octave above C on the keyboard is the next C up, and similarly, an octave below C is the next C down.

Pitch

The "highness" or "lowness" of a sound. Pitches are determined by the frequency of a sound—a middle C on the piano is usually tuned to 256 Hz (Hertz; cycles per second). Pitches are usually referred to by letter names (e.g., C, D, E) or by solfege names (e.g., do, ray, mi), though, and not by frequency. (People say "give me an A", not "give me a 440 Hz".) (See *duration*.)

Pizzicato

A term used in relation to bowed stringed instruments (like violins and 'cellos, but not guitars) which means plucked with the fingers. In other words, instead of using a bow, the musician plucks the string, usually with one of the fingers of the right hand.

Retrograde

Taking a melody or a chunk of a melody and playing it backwards.

Scale

The notes of a key, arranged in sequence. (See *major* and *minor*.)

Semi-tone

On the keyboard, the distance from one key to the nearest next key. That is, if you start on the white note C, a semi-tone above would be the black note C♯, while a semi-tone below would be the note B.

Sharp

A sign (♯) placed before a note, indicating that the note to be sung or played is a semi-tone higher than the note. On the keyboard, this kind of accidental most often applies to the black keys. In English, this means that a G♯ is the black key immediately to the right, i.e., above, the white note G.

Solid Form

When all of the notes of a chord (e.g., C, E, G) are played or sung at once, the chord is said to be in solid form. (See *broken form*.)

Staff

The five horizontal lines used to notate music in standard notation. Generally, one instrument, one voice, or one hand in the case of keyboard instruments, is notated along a staff line. When more than one set of staff lines is joined at the left by a bracket, (e.g., two staff lines for the right and left hands for keyboard instruments) the result is called the Grand Staff.

Suite

Usually refers to a collection of instrumental pieces of a dance-like character, typical of the Baroque Period (around 1600–1750). The collection of pieces in a Suite most often used by Bach included five movements: (1) Allemande, (2) Courante, (3) Saraband, a (4) Minuet, Passepied, Gavotte, Bouree, Polonaise, Anglaise, Loure, or Air, and (5) ending with a Gigue. There are other musical forms belonging to the later Classical Period (e.g., Sonata, Sonatina) and the Romantic Period (e.g., Nocturne) that are mentioned in the book as well. But to list them all would take another book, so I'll stop here!

Tempo

The speed at which a piece should be played. In some cases, an M.M. appears at the beginning of a composition indicating the speed or tempo. (M.M. actually stands for Maelzel's Metronome ...Maelzel was a person.) Thus, if the marking is M.M. ♩ = 144, then the tempo would be 144 quarter notes per minute. People use metronomes—little machines that click away at the speed you set— to keep to a certain tempo.

Tenor Clef

A marking at the beginning of a line of music indicating the relative pitches of each note on the staff. The tenor clef, also known as a C clef, has two brackets which surround the line for the note C. The notes falling within the tenor clef are in the mid-range of pitches, corresponding to tenor vocal music, 'cello string music, and so on. The tenor clef is less often used than the soprano and bass clefs, probably because fewer people are accustomed to reading the tenor clef, so much modern vocal music for tenors is written in the treble clef. Also, a good deal of 'cello music conveniently falls within the bass clef range. (See also *alto clef, treble clef,* and *bass clef.*)

Time Signature

A mark, consisting of two numbers or a single sign, near the beginning of the piece, indicating the meter. For simple time signatures, the top number indicates the number of beats in a measure, the bottom number indicates the value or duration of the beat. For example, 2/4 time means that there are two beats in a bar, and a quarter note gets the beat. In 4/4 time, there are four beats in a bar, and again, a quarter note gets the beat. In 3/8 time, there are three beats in a bar, and an eighth note gets the beat. Sometimes letters mark the time signature (e.g., a C indicating common or 4/4 time). Some time signatures, such as 6/8 time, are compound, and slightly more complicated to describe. In 6/8 time, for example, there are two beats in a bar, and a dotted quarter note (equal to 3 eighth notes) gets the beat. If you have trouble understanding this, don't worry about it. A lot of theory students have trouble with it too.

Tone

The distance made up of two semi-tones. On a keyboard, a tone above C would be D (skipping over the C♯ in between). A tone below C, on the other hand, would be the note B♭ since one semi-tone below would be the white note B, two semi-tones below takes us to the next black note, i.e., B♭.

Tonic

The home key of a piece of music, or, the first note of the scale of the key in which a piece of music is written. Just as "all roads lead to home," all notes (eventually) lead home to the tonic note.

Transposition

Moving all of the notes of a composition up or down a fixed interval (distance), so that the piece is in a new key. For example, if *Twinkle, Twinkle, Little Star* was originally played in the key of C (as in Figure 1–6), and then moved up a fifth to G, and played in the new key of G, the piece would have been transposed up a perfect fifth. The result of the transposition is that the composition still sounds the same, that is, can be identified as *Twinkle, Twinkle, Little Star*, except that the whole thing, in this example, sounds higher.

Treble Clef

A marking at the beginning of a line of music indicating the relative pitches of each note on the staff. The treble clef, also known as the G clef, has a "curl" around the line for the note G. The notes falling within the treble clef are high, corresponding to soprano vocal music, violin string music, and so on. (See also *bass clef, alto clef,* and *tenor clef.*)

Walking Bass

Refers to a lower part in blues music where notes are played one after another as if the fingers were walking up the keyboard. usually each chord has four notes (e.g. the four notes C, E♭, F, G would be a possible walking bass for the C minor chord), and the chord progression is often made up of twelve chords—I, I, I, I, IV, IV, I, I, V, IV, I, I; where each of the Roman numerals refers to a chord relative to the home key. That is, "I" refers to the chord built on the tonic, "IV" refers to the chord built on the fourth chord, and "V" refers to the chord built on the fifth chord. The example of a walking bass given in Figure 5–16 is a walking bass for blues in C.

References

Altwerger, B., C. Edelsky, & B. M. Flores. 1987. Whole Language: What's New? *The Reading Teacher*, 41, 144–154.

Armstrong, M. 1981. *Closely Observed Children: The Diary of a Primary Classroom*. New York: Cameleon Education.

Atwell, N. 1987. *In the Middle: Writing, Reading, and Learning with Adolescents*. Portsmouth, N.H.: Boynton–Cook.

Baker, A., & J. Baker. 1990. *Mathematics in Process*. Portsmouth, N.H.: Heinemann.

Bamberger, J. 1982. Revisiting Children's Drawings of Simple Rhythms: A Function of Reflection-in-Action. In S. Strauss (Ed.) *U-Shaped Behavioral Growth*. New York: Academic Press.

Bamberger, J., & D. Schön. 1980. The Figural-Formal Transaction. DSRE Working Paper #1, Cambridge, Massachusetts: Massachusetts Institute of Technology.

Bateson, M. C. 1989. *Composing a Life*. New York: Penguin.

Belenky, M. F., B. M. Clinchy, N. R. Goldberger, & J. M. Tarule. 1986. *Women's Ways of Knowing*. New York: Basic Books.

Bissex, G.. 1980. GNYS AT WRK: *A Child Learns to Write and Read*. Cambridge, Mass: Harvard University Press.

BORSTAD, J. 1989. *But I've Been Pouring Sounds All Day*. Presented at the annual meeting of the Canadian Society for the Study of Education (CSSE), Quebec City, Quebec, Canada.

BORSTAD, J. 1990. *But I've Been Pouring Sounds All Day*. Unpublished master's thesis, Faculty of Education, Queen's University, Kingston, Ontario, Canada.

BRUNER, J. 1990. *Acts of Meaning*. Cambridge, Mass.: Harvard University Press.

CALKINS, L. M. 1983. *Lessons from a Child: On the Teaching and Learning of Writing*. Portsmouth, N.H.: Heinemann.

CALKINS, L. M. 1986. *The Art of Teaching Writing*. Portsmouth, N.H.: Heinemann.

CONNELLY, F. M., & D. J. CLANDININ. 1988. *Teachers as Curriculum Planners: Narratives of Experience*. Toronto: OISE Press.

DALCROZE, E. 1912. *The Eurythmics of Jacques-Dalcroze*. London: Constable & Co.

DALCROZE, E. 1921. *Rhythm, Music, and Education*. London: Putnam's Sons.

DAVIDSON, L., & L. SCRIPP. 1988a. Young Children's Musical Representations: Windows on Music Cognition. In J. Sloboda (Ed.), *Generative Processes in Music: The Psychology of Performance, Improvisation, and Composition* (pp. 195–230). New York: Oxford University Press.

DAVIDSON, L., & L. SCRIPP. 1988b. Education and development in music from a cognitive perspective. In C. Hargreaves (Ed.). *Children and the Arts* (pp. 59–86). London: Open University Press.

DAVIDSON, L., L. SCRIPP, & P. WELSH. 1988. Happy Birthday: Evidence for Conflicts of Perceptual Knowledge and Conceptual Understanding. *Journal of Aesthetic Education, 22*, 65–74.

DEWEY, J. 1902. *The Child and the Curriculum*. Chicago: University of Chicago Press.

DONALDSON, M. 1980. *Children's Minds*. Glasgow: Fontana/William Collins and Sons.

EGNATOFF, W. J. 1989. An Hour of a Thousand Discoveries. Unpublished manuscript, Queen's University, Kingston, Ontario.

FALBEL, A. 1989. *Friskolen 70: An Ethnographically Informed Inquiry Into the Social Context of Learning*. Unpublished doctoral thesis, Learning and Epistemology Group, Media Lab, Massachusetts Institute of Technology, Cambridge, Massachusetts.

GALE, R. 1990. *Teaching Music Across the Curriculum*. Unpublished master's thesis. Faculty of Education, Queen's University, Kingston, Ontario.

GARDNER, H. 1983. *Frames of Mind: The Theory of Multiple Intelligences*. New York: Basic Books.

GENTRY, J. R. 1982. An Analysis of Developmental Spelling in GNYS AT WRK. *The Reading Teacher*, 36 (2), 192–200.

GILLIGAN, C. 1982. *In a Different Voice*. Cambridge, Mass.: Harvard University Press.

GOODMAN, K. S. 1986. *What's Whole in Whole Language?* Richmond Hill, Ontario: Scholastic.

GOODMAN, N. 1969. *The Languages of Art*. New York: Oxford University Press.

GRAVES, D. 1983. *Writing: Teachers and Children at Work*. Portsmouth, N. H.: Heinemann.

GROUT, D. J. 1960. *A History of Western Music*. New York: W.W. Norton.

HAWKINS, D. 1974. *The Informed Vision*. New York: Agathon Press.

HILDEBRANDT, C. 1985. *A Developmental Study of Children's Representations of Simple Rhythms*. Unpublished doctoral thesis, Department of Psychology, University of California, Berkeley, California.

HODGKIN, R. A. 1985. *Playing and Exploring: Education Through the Discovery of Order*. London: Methuen.

HOLT, J. 1967, 1983. *How Children Learn*. New York: Dell.

HOLT, J. 1976. *Instead of Education*. New York: E.P. Dutton.

JUNG, C. G. 1946. *Psychological Types*. London: Kegan Paul, Trench, & Trubner.

LANGER, S. *Philosophy in a New Key: Studies in the Symbolism of Reason, Rite, and Art*. Cambridge, Mass.: Harvard University Press.

LINTON, P. 1991. *The Effects of Text on Children's Invented Notations of Melody*. Unpublished Honours Psychology thesis, Queen's University, Kingston, Ontario.

MILLS, H. & J. A. CLYDE. 1990. *Portraits of Whole Language Classrooms: Learning for All Ages*. Portsmouth, N.H.: Heinemann.

MURRAY, D. 1985. *A Writer Teaches Writing*. 2nd ed. Boston, Mass.: Houghton Mifflin.

NEWMAN, J. (Ed.). 1983. *Whole Language: Translating Theory Into Practice*. Portsmouth, N.H.: Heinemann.

NEWMAN, J., & S. CHURCH. 1990. Myths of Whole Language. *The Reading Teacher*, 44, 20–26.

NEWMAN, D., P. GRIFFIN, & M. COLE. 1989. *The Construction Zone: Working for Cognitive Change in School*. New York: Cambridge University Press.

OSBORNE, R., & P. FREYBERG. 1985. *Learning in Science: The Implications of Children's Science*. Portsmouth, N.H.: Heinemann.

PAPERT, S. 1980. *Mindstorms: Children, Computers, and Powerful Ideas*. New York: Basic Books.

PIAGET, J. 1941, 1965. *The Child's Conception of Number*. New York: W.W. Norton.

———. 1947, 1981. *The Psychology of Intelligence*. Totowa, N.J.: Littlefield, Adams, & Co.

———. 1952. *The Origins of Intelligence in Children*. New York: International Universities Press, Inc.

———. 1955, 1974. *The Language and Thought of the Child*. New York: Meridian Books.

———. 1962. *Play, Dreams and Imitation in Childhood*. New York: W.W. Norton.

POLANYI, M. 1958. *Personal Knowledge: Towards a Post Critical Philosophy*. London: Routledge & Kegan Paul.

POLKINGHORNE, D. E. 1988. *Narrative Knowing and the Human Sciences*. Albany, N.Y.: State University of New York Press.

RANDEL, D. M. 1978. *Harvard Concise Dictionary of Music*. Cambridge, Mass.: Harvard University Press.

RASTALL, R. 1982. *The Notation of Western Music*. New York: St. Martin's Press.

SCHAFER, R. M. 1975. *The Rhinoceros in the Classroom*. Toronto: Universal Edition.

SCHÖN, D. A. 1983. *The Reflective Practitioner: How Professionals Think in Action*. New York: Basic Books.

SERVICE, R. 1907, 1986. *The Cremation of Sam McGee*. Toronto: Kids Can Press.

SMITH, K. C. 1989. *The Representation and Reproduction of Musical Rhythm by Children and Adults*. Unpublished doctoral thesis, Department of Psychology, Queen's University, Kingston, Ontario.

SWANWICK, K., & J. TILLMAN. 1986. The Sequence of Musical Development: A Study of Children's Compositions. *British Journal of Music Education*, 3 (3), 305–339.

UPITIS, R. 1983. Keeping the Pulse: Lessons from LogoMusic. *Presented at the Educational Computing Organization of Ontario Conference*, Toronto, Ontario.

———. 1985. *Children's Understanding of Rhythm: The Relationship*

Between Development and Music Training. Unpublished doctoral thesis, Harvard University, Cambridge, Massachusetts. (Available on University Microfilms International, Ann Arbor, Michigan.)

————. 1987a. Children's Understanding of Rhythm: The Relationship Between Development and Music Training. *Psychomusicology*, 7 (1), 41–61.

————. 1987b. A Child's Development of Notation Through Composition: A Case Study. *Arts and Learning Research*, 5 (1), 102–119.

————. 1989. The Craft of Composition: Helping Children Create Music with Computer Tools. *Psychomusicology*, 8 (2), 85–96.

————. 1990a. Children's Invented Notations of Familiar and Unfamiliar Melodies. *Psychomusicology*, 9 (1), 89–106.

————. 1990b. *This Too Is Music*. Portsmouth, N.H.: Heinemann.

VYGOTSKY, L. 1934, 1962, 1986. *Thought and Language*. Cambridge, Mass.: MIT Press.

WALLACE, N. 1990. *Child's Work: Taking Children's Choices Seriously*. Boston, Mass.: Holt Associates.

WELLS, G. 1986. *The Meaning Makers*. Portsmouth, N.H.: Heinemann.

WHITEHEAD, A. N. 1929. *The Aims of Education*. New York: Macmillan.

WHITIN, D. J., H. MILLS, & T. O'KEEFE. 1990. *Living and Learning Mathematics*. Portsmouth, N.H.: Heinemann.